ARE WE
READY
—FOR—
JESUS?

ARE WE
READY
—FOR—
JESUS?

How to Prepare for
His Return

NELSON WALTERS

SERAPHINA PRESS • MINNEAPOLIS, MN

Copyright © 2015 by Nelson Walters

SERAPHINA
PRESS

Seraphina Press
322 First Avenue N, 5th floor
Minneapolis, MN 55401
612.455.2293
www.SeraphinaPress.com

www.thegospelintheendtimes.com

ISBN-13: 978-1-63413-492-7
LCCN: 2015906275

Distributed by Itasca Books

Cover Design by Sophie Chi
Typeset by D. Umbridge

Printed in the United States of America

Join the movement to awaken the Church:

Ready for Jesus Ministries
www.AreWeReadyForJesus.com
nelson@AreWeReadyForJesus.com

ACKNOWLEDGMENTS

First and foremost, I give all praise and honor to my Savior and Lord of my life, Jesus Christ, who twenty-two years ago had mercy on a wretch like me, and raised me from death to life in him. Jesus, you are my wonderful counselor, my mighty God, my everlasting Father, and my prince of peace. You are the inspiration for every word in this book and every breath that I take. I long for the day when faith shall be sight and when you will come with great glory on the clouds of heaven. We will fly into your arms and forever be together!

Laura, you are God's greatest gift to me. You are my perfect helper whose strengths complement my weaknesses. You are beautiful in every way. Thank you for enduring and putting up with me during this journey of writing. Only you and I know what a sacrifice it was on your part. I love you.

Mark Davidson, you are my brother in the Lord. You have taught me so much about writing and friendship. Thank you for being a companion through the development of my ministry. It would be nothing without your help. God placed you on my path.

Joel Richardson, you have been an amazing encouragement to me. Thank you for having the courage to listen to the Holy Spirit when the entire world believed something else, and for continuing to have the courage to announce that the Antichrist will be Islamic to a nation that grows ever more politically correct. Thank you for teaching me through your writings. I love your heart for the lost and for Israel.

Joseph Lenard and Donald Zoller, you both share my passion for the Lord's kingdom and an uncanny similarity of vision. Thank you for your tireless devotion to this project and Godly insight. Your dedicated efforts made this book both richer and more readable. Most of all, thank you for your friendship.

Mike Ashcraft, eight years ago God called us to move to North Carolina to sit under your teaching. I praise God for your shepherd's heart and your willingness to listen to our Father. In 2014 I leaned on My One Word, *focus*, and our corporate word, *risk*. This book was the result. My One Word 2015 is *radical*. Let's see what God will do.

My couples small group at PC3, you are our family.

Cory, "the effective prayer of a righteous man can accomplish much" (James 5:16 NASB). You prayed and look at the outcome. The effective prayer of a righteous sixth-grader accomplishes much as well.

All those who read and critiqued this book, thank you for your wonderful heart for Jesus and your insight. This book is so much richer because of it. I praise God for brothers and sisters like you.

All the readers of my blog, *The Gospel in the End Times*, and my yokefellows at *Ready for Jesus Ministries*, together we will not be afraid, and we will "drink from our hands." God willing we will help awaken the churches.

PRAISE FOR

ARE WE READY FOR JESUS?

Are We Ready for Jesus? is a truly fantastic and insightful end-time manifesto for the last-days Church. So many books discuss what the author thinks will occur in the last days, but so few discuss how the Church should be responding. This book is a much-needed work, giving solid pastoral application to several of the most important themes found in the end-times scriptures. I cannot more highly recommend this book to all those who desire to walk through the days ahead in a manner worthy of Christ.

—**Joel Richardson**, *New York Times* best-selling author of *Mideast Beast*

Are We Ready For Jesus? is a must read for all Christians. The Church today mostly treats Christ's return as irrelevant or distant with no direct application to the way we live our lives today. *Are We Ready* shows us the meaning of Christ's commands to "watch" and to be ready for his return. The end times are not what we thought they were. You owe it to yourself, your family, and your local church to understand the truths in this book. It is high time we wake up!

—**Mark Davidson**, Author of *Daniel Revisited: Discovering the Four Mideast Signs Leading to the Antichrist*

Are We Ready For Jesus? is an eye-opening revelation, with practical application. Nelson Walters' message grips the heart and brings a fresh understanding to the end days. Never before in history has the Church so urgently needed to understand the prophetic scriptures. There is no doubt in my mind that God is going to use this work to powerfully awaken this generation with renewed zeal for Christ's return. The Church needs this message, and every believer in Christ needs this book!

—**John Preacher**, Director of *Armageddon News*

God is doing a new thing—*unsealing* understanding of His prophetic scriptures. Many of us see and feel this. Nelson Walters has been obedient to the leading of the Holy Spirit and has written *Are We Ready for Jesus?*—a book to help awaken the Church and teach us *how* to *get ready* for Jesus' second coming. Nelson gives new insight into the end-times teaching of Jesus' Olivet Discourse and reveals unique understanding of four parables Jesus used to convey end-times messages on *how* the Church needs to prepare for His coming. The Holy Spirit has revealed these understandings because the time to prepare has come. We highly recommend Nelson's book. This teaching is a *game changer* in many ways. The message needs to resound within America's churches and in churches around the world.

—**Joseph Lenard** and **Donald Zoller**, co-authors of *The Last Shofar!— What the Fall Feasts of the Lord Are Telling the Church* (2014)

Are We Ready for Jesus? has performed an enormous service for the body of Christ. Pastors and church leaders need to be presented with it, learn, and then ACT on it. "If you know these things, you are blessed if you do them." Christianity has never been a passive exercise, and especially not now in the terminal generation. Read this book, and you will see it proven scripturally that if you think the next prophetic event to occur is Jesus coming, you are in a deep, dark slumber and you need to awake before it is too late . . . for you and the flock you lead. The time for compromise and laziness is over.

—**Christopher Mantei**, *WingsOfTheEagle.com*, Voice of the Martyrs

Nelson Walters' missionary emphasis in *Are We Ready for Jesus?* captures the New Testament spirit, emphasis, and impetus while also remaining practical and simple. The gospel message is not complicated and is not merely a theological exercise. Mr. Walters keeps the focus where it should be and reminds us of the simple truths contained and commanded therein. The hard part will be how you choose to respond.

—**Joshua Stateham**, Youth With A Mission (YWAM), Network for Strategic Initiatives

The return of Jesus to rule the earth from Jerusalem is one of the most misunderstood and neglected principles of scripture. The Holy Spirit is raising up voices throughout the world to wake up the Church and to prepare her for what lies ahead. Nelson Walters is one of these voices, and *Are We Ready for Jesus?* may well be one of the most important books that Christians will read during this season of preparation.

—**Greg Maxwell**, *The Issachar Mandate* Blog

Are We Ready for Jesus? is a simple and yet revolutionary wake-up call to Christians, who for the most part, are asleep concerning the end times. Being a person born in another country and currently living in the US, I follow church trends in both the US and my native country. I can tell that Christians are asleep not only in America but also in other parts of the world, and that is due to end-time misconceptions which I call *end-time fairy tales*. This book will address those misconceptions and help you understand why the Church is for the most part asleep and help equip you to bring a wake-up call to Christians everywhere.

—**Rodrigo Silva**, author of *The Coming Bible Prophecy Reformation: Shifting from the European to the Middle Eastern End Time Paradigm*

CONTENTS

CHAPTER ONE

READY OR NOT

Those who were *ready went* in with him to the wedding feast; and the door was shut. Later the other virgins also came, saying, "Lord, lord, open up for us." But he answered, "Truly I say to you, I do not know you." (Matthew 25:10–12 NASB, emphasis mine)

Life is full of major events and challenges for which we have to prepare. Some spend months or years preparing for a wedding, the SAT exams, or the launch of a new business. For others, getting ready for Christmas each year is a yeoman's task of baking, cleaning, buying, and decorating.

Establishing a dental clinic in Ghana, West Africa, was a major challenge for me. After shipping equipment halfway around the world, I found the entire nation of Ghana had only one dental equipment technician! Sometimes life takes us by surprise, and we must adapt our preparations.

Most Americans have spent countless hours getting ready for life's challenges, but the vast majority of us haven't even considered preparing for the most important day ever: Jesus's return.

Are you ready for Jesus to return? Is your church ready? What does ready *even* mean? When we ask these questions, Christians usually respond with a mix of fear, apathy, and confusion. Let's look at a couple of typical American responses:

- We don't know when he's coming, so why prepare?

- Even though this might sound sacrilegious, I'd rather he waited a little longer until after my grandchildren are born. Oh, and maybe after I have a chance to visit Hawaii. Then I guess I'll be ready.

- I go to church every Sunday. My pastor doesn't say anything about getting ready.

- I am sick and tired of what is happening in America. I am good and ready for Jesus to set things right. (Liberals and conservatives both answer this the same way!)

- I've asked Jesus into my heart, so I guess I'm ready. That's all I need, right?

People are uncertain about what being ready for Jesus really means. There are so many aspects: emotional, spiritual, and physical preparation. The term being *ready* means different things to different people. What matters most, of course, is what ready means to Jesus.

My first pastor had a favorite saying: "The main thing is to keep the main thing the main thing." I like that. Focus on what is most important. This book details what Jesus told us was important about preparing for his glorious return. You may have read other books about the second coming, but this one is different. Some give an opinion of the chronology of future events. Others attempt to show how current events are related to prophecy. This book begins with the prophetic word, but then shows how to apply it. It discusses how to respond and react to the prophecies. In my opinion, this was Jesus's intent. He gave us prophecy so that we could understand the times and respond appropriately. In this light of application, every one of Jesus's teachings about his return takes on new meaning and is a game changer. After reading this book, hopefully you will never think about his return the same way again.

THE PREDOMINANT VIEW OF THE CHURCH

The majority in the American Church today hold the simplistic view that everyone who has made a profession of faith in Jesus is ready for his return. Most believe that this profession alone is all that is needed. I used to believe that myself. I've been a disciple of Jesus for twenty-two years. There was a time when I was tired of hearing about his return. What is more controversial than prophecy? If you want to see Christians embarrass themselves or start arguing as if they were talking politics, just mention the timing of the rapture! Everyone has an opinion and is quick to voice it. I wondered, *Why does this even matter? Isn't* winning souls the most important thing we can do as we wait for Christ's return? Does it really matter what happens after Christians are with Jesus in heaven? Isn't the key presenting the gospel to as many folks as possible to get them into heaven? Can't we avoid that end-time stuff?

I also wondered if all those folks who talked about prophecy were a little strange. Some are like Chicken Little—always seeing *the end* in every international happening. And isn't this prophecy business dangerous? If not handled correctly, teaching about Jesus's return can scare some churchgoers, especially seekers. Do we really want to stunt church growth?

If any of that describes your thinking, this is the right book for you. Those thoughts are exactly where I started out ten years ago when God took me on this journey.

Now, obviously, the conversion from spiritual death to life that occurs at salvation is *the* most important and foundational aspect of preparing for Christ's return. We can't minimize it. This book discusses this fundamental aspect of preparation in chapter four: It's a Wedding. But, as I matured as a Christian and carefully studied the scriptures, it was apparent that 25% of the Bible involves Jesus's return. I asked myself, *Isn't it logical to conclude that there is more to being prepared than just a profession of faith?* If not, God wasted a lot of pages giving us unnecessary details. It was this internal conflict between what I was being taught in church and what my personal Bible study was uncovering that launched me on this journey of discovery.

OTHER CLUES

Other clues in scripture lead me to conclude that preparation for Jesus's return involves more than a profession of faith. His primary teachings on his return are contained in what is called the Olivet Discourse in Matthew 24 and 25, Mark 13, and Luke 21. At the conclusion of this teaching, Jesus instructs us, in the form of five parables, how to apply his prophetic message. These parables imply a much greater level of preparation than what I had been previously taught. Here are excerpts from the parables:

> If the head of the house had known at what time of the night the thief was coming, he would have been on the alert and would not have allowed his house to be broken into. For this reason you also must be ready . . . Who then is the faithful and sensible slave whom his master put in charge of his household to give them their food at the proper time? Blessed is that slave whom his master finds so doing when he comes. Truly I say to you that he will put him in charge of all his possessions. (Matthew 24:43–47 NASB)

> Those who were ready went in with him to the wedding feast; and the door was shut. Later the other virgins also came, saying, "Lord, lord, open up for us." But he answered, "Truly I say to you, I do not know you." (Matthew 25:10–12 NASB)

> His master said to him, "Well done, good and faithful slave. You were faithful with a few things, I will put you in charge of many things; enter into the joy of your master." (Matthew 25:21 NASB)

> For to everyone who has, more shall be given, and he will have an abundance; but from the one who does not have, even what he does have shall be taken away. Throw out the worthless slave into the outer darkness; in that place there will be weeping and gnashing of teeth. (Matthew 25:29–31 NASB)

These passages suggest that rewards, punishment, and even eternal separation from God await churchgoers based on their preparation. From these verses it's obvious that being ready for Jesus's return is of eternal importance. It is also more complex than what the Church has considered. This book goes into great depth in explaining what Jesus means by being ready.

YOU MEAN WE *AREN'T* READY?

How is it possible that we aren't ready? The Church has had two thousand years to ponder the red letters—what Jesus said—in the Bible. The greatest Christian thinkers of all time have written on this topic. Could they be mistaken?

Yes, unfortunately. This is an incredibly hard concept to comprehend. Does this mean this book is an authority and they are not? Heaven forbid! Many of these men and women were supremely intelligent and led mightily by God's Spirit. Jesus, however, was aware we would *all* lose our focus on his return and misinterpret his teachings. Two thousand years ago he prophesied that we would fall asleep. In the next chapter we will explain this phenomenon in detail and how it has led to a misunderstanding of his return. Hopefully, this book will help us return to Jesus's clear and direct instructions. It is time to wake up, fix our eyes on him, and prepare.

THE OLIVET DISCOURSE

We will be looking at Jesus's teachings throughout the four Gospels and Revelation. His primary teaching about his return, however, is in a section of scripture known as the Olivet Discourse. Jesus gave this sermon on one of the last afternoons before he was betrayed. He had just had a heated exchange with the established Jewish leaders in Jerusalem. As our Lord and his disciples left the temple area, the disciples were stunned by the interchange they had just witnessed. They tried to break the tension by commenting on the majestic temple architecture, but Jesus rebuffed them by saying that soon not one of those magnificent stones would stand upon another.

On their way back to their "camp" on the Mount of Olives, Jesus's disciples tried to put the day's events in perspective. After his triumphant entry into Jerusalem on Palm Sunday, they had expected Jesus to be recognized as Messiah and king. Now everything was falling apart. Jesus and the leaders of the nation had just had a knockdown war of words from which there was no going back. Not only that, Jesus had just prophesied that the temple, where the Messiah would someday sit as king, would soon be destroyed. How could Jesus be crowned king after that day's events? Their vision of the future had been smashed into a million pieces like the temple stones in Jesus's prophecy.

I can imagine Jesus's closest disciples whispering under their breath, *If Jesus isn't going to become king, what will happen to us?* They finally got up the nerve to ask their master about the future. Jesus responded with the Olivet Discourse, an amazing prophetic sermon about his return.

You and I aren't that much different from the disciples. Those of Jesus's day were clueless about what was about to happen during his first coming—the years from his birth to his resurrection and ascension. We are fairly clueless about the events about to take place before Jesus's second coming. His teaching on that April evening is even more relevant to us today than it was for the disciples. We are about to live it out!

READING THIS BOOK

If you aren't sure about Jesus yet, thank you for reading. It takes a lot of guts to read a Christian book if you don't yet believe. Hopefully, it will show you the amazing detail God has planned for the return of his Son. I have already prayed for you. I prayed that when you begin to see the events we discuss in this little book come true, you will be cut to the heart and realize that Jesus truly is the Son of God.

I also recommend that you read the outstanding book *The Case for Christ* by Lee Strobel (Zondervan, 1988). In it, Strobel makes an airtight case for the divinity of Jesus. I am sure you will find that book interesting as you seek the truth.

If you are already a Christian, that is awesome. Thank you for reading as well. It takes intestinal fortitude to read a book that may be a bit different and challenging. I have prayed that you are able to read it with an open mind. If you are, it may change your life.

You have chosen the wrong paperback if you are looking for a book by an author with an academic degree or by someone famous. I'm an unlikely choice to write a book, but God frequently chooses unlikely persons to do his work. The weak, the unattractive, the uneducated, and the meek can all fit God's requirements if we simply listen and obey.

I am positive Jesus didn't give us the revelations in this book for us to use solely for our personal salvation and edification. He is communicating them so unlikely candidates such as you and I can share his Word with other unlikely choices. As you read this book, pray; and ask the Holy Spirit how he wants you to share this information. When you pray for guidance, the Holy Spirit may ask you to help awaken the Church. Don't be scared if you feel led to do something you don't feel completely comfortable doing. That is a sure sign the answer is from God! He chooses the unlikely and equips us to accomplish what we are inadequate to achieve on our own. All he needs from you (and me) is obedience.

SUMMARY

We have seen that there is a great deal of confusion about what being ready for Jesus's return entails. The predominant view of the Church is that all that is needed is to have made a profession of faith. Based on this belief, the Church has focused nearly all of its preparation on evangelism. Scripture gives us tantalizing clues, however, that preparation is much more involved than the current position of the Church.

The basic steps for getting ready for Jesus from this chapter are:

> **1. Preparing for Jesus's return is more complex than imagined:**
> We need to open our hearts and minds for what Jesus wants to teach us.

In the next chapter we will learn the Church is asleep, and the devastating implications that slumber will have on churchgoers.

I invite you to spend an evening with what Jesus wants to teach his Church. I don't have it all figured out; I'm seeking God's truth just like you. But maybe after you finish this book, you will also feel compelled to help prepare the Church: your church. There is more at stake than I ever imagined when I began this journey. Let's find out about it together.

CHAPTER TWO

THE EMPEROR'S NEW CLOTHES:

WHY AREN'T WE READY?

But be sure of this, that if the head of the house had known at what time of the night the thief was coming, he would have been on the alert and would not have allowed his house to be broken into. For this reason you also must be *ready*; for the Son of Man is coming at an hour when you do not think He will. (Matthew 24:43–44 NASB, emphasis mine)

Most radio stations in this country no longer feature live DJs. For the most part, stations play a prerecorded program, including the DJ's banter and preselected music. Many times a corporation hundreds of miles away records the programming. These prerecorded programs can result in awkward situations. Nashville, Tennessee, experienced one of the most severe floods in its history a few years back. While the Cumberland River was destroying numerous historic Nashville landmarks, nearly every radio station featured a DJ saying, *Welcome to Music City, USA. It's a beautiful day in Nashville!* The radio stations were completely disconnected from the reality outside their windows.

Recently, my wife met with one of her good friends. This friend was anxious about the state of the world. "Everyone seems to know something big is about to happen," she said. "Why isn't my church talking about it? Our family got together last night and agreed to meet on my uncle's farm if the power goes out and never comes back on."

Many Christians wonder why we aren't discussing Jesus's return. Why do we seem disconnected from the reality right outside our stained-glass windows? More people are asking those questions in pews across the country than many pastors or elders would admit. Jesus's return is the elephant in the sanctuary. Everyone is thinking about it, but inside our churches no one is talking about it. Why is that?

Jesus has already given us the answer. In the parable of the ten virgins in Matthew 25, he tells us most of us are fast asleep. You read that correctly. Jesus prophesied that the majority of the Christian Church would be slumbering before his return. If you haven't heard this teaching before, it can be shocking news.

> At that time [just prior to Jesus's return] the kingdom of heaven will be like ten virgins who took their lamps and went out to meet the bridegroom. Five of them were foolish and five were wise. The foolish ones took their lamps but did not take any oil with them. The wise ones, however, took oil in jars along with their lamps. The bridegroom was a long time in coming *and they all became drowsy and fell asleep.* (Matthew 25:1–5 NIV, emphasis and clarification mine)

The first thing you probably noticed in the parable is that Jesus didn't say 50 percent or 90 percent of the virgins were asleep. He said *all ten* of the virgins were asleep. You might expect the foolish virgins to be caught napping, but even the wise virgins were sleeping. You may never have heard this parable taught this way before. That's because in regard to Jesus's return, most of us are asleep and we have missed the point! That's a flippant answer, but it is close to the truth. A more complete answer is that Jesus's teaching doesn't match our theology. We think highly of ourselves. We like to believe we have his return all figured out. Jesus's words tell us we don't understand his return at all.

IT'S A GAME CHANGER IF THE CHURCH IS ASLEEP.

If Jesus is correct and the Church is asleep, it means everything about how we view the return of Christ needs to be reexamined.

- We may be missing prophetic events happening right before our eyes.

- We may be misunderstanding what Jesus wants us to accomplish in these days before his return.

- We may be misinterpreting scripture and leading ourselves and our fellow churchgoers astray.

Being accused of being asleep is serious. It would mean most seminary professors, denomination presidents, pastors, prophecy teachers, elders, and most of us sitting in the pews on Sundays are snoozing regarding Jesus's return. It would mean we don't fully understand the return of our king.

You can instantly see why the majority of the Church would not want to deal with the implications of this passage of scripture. It is the *Emperor's New Clothes* of the Bible. If Jesus is correct, we are deluding ourselves that we understand his return when we really don't.

WHAT OTHERS ARE SAYING

Everyone reading and interpreting the first five verses of the parable of the ten virgins has to make one of two choices. We either have to accept Jesus's clear and simple teaching at face value, or we must convince ourselves that the parable doesn't apply to the Church. There is no other option. Because of this, many have desperately searched for an explanation that would spiritualize Jesus's simple message. Before we move on, let's look at these interpretations and examine the arguments made by those who don't believe this teaching applies to the Church.

Some teach that the virgins in the parable are Jewish. This can't be correct. First, please note that all the virgins were going to meet their bridegroom. Jews are not looking for a bridegroom; they are waiting for a king/messiah. Christians are waiting for Jesus, who is our bridegroom. This parable is not about those outside of the Church.

In a similar manner, some in the Church teach that the entire Olivet Discourse, where the parable of the ten virgins is found, is only for and about the Jews. Jesus did not specify that the Olivet Discourse was to apply only to the Jews. He taught this sermon in the same manner and at approximately the same time as he gave his disciples other teachings like the great commission (Matthew 28:18–20) and the upper room discourse (John 13–17). All three of these teachings were meant to edify the Church. All were given without specifics as to being applied to the Church or to the Jews. If Jesus meant the Olivet Discourse to apply only to the Jews, he would have said so plainly. He did not. He didn't even hint that it applied only to them.

In addition, there is overwhelming evidence from the early Church (first and second century) that they believed the Olivet Discourse applied to the Christian Church. The most currently revered, noncanonical document from this period is the *Didache*, an ancient Greek document thought to predate the book of Revelation. It was possibly written as early as 50 AD. This document is thought to be the direct teachings of the apostles, and acted as a doctrinal statement for early churches prior to the assembly of the modern canon. Many of its sections parallel the Olivet Discourse word-for-word and concept-by-concept. This ancient document clearly demonstrates that the early Church believed that Jesus's teaching in Matthew 24 and 25 applied to them.[1]

Returning to the parable of the ten virgins, others teach it is about Christians who come to faith after the tribulation period has begun. That is impossible because the virgins are asleep. Anyone who teaches that persecuted saints are asleep obviously hasn't faced much persecution!

It is evident from this analysis that this parable and the Olivet Discourse are meant to edify us, current-day churchgoers; we all need to pay special attention to these teachings.

WHAT WOULD A SLEEPING CHURCH LOOK LIKE?

Let's test the theory that the Church is asleep. If we *are* sleeping, what would our churches look like?

- Few churches would openly discuss the return of Jesus on a regular basis.

- Some would claim opposing theories of Jesus's return are too controversial and so would avoid them.

- Some would view discussing or preaching the return of Jesus as irrelevant because they believe we won't see any difficult times prior to his return.

- Some would view discussing the return of Jesus as an issue that's secondary to social issues like AIDS, same-sex marriage, or human trafficking.

- Churches would spend the majority of their monies on church events rather than missions done in the name of Jesus, and attempting to reach the lost.

- Churchgoers would live earthly lives concentrating on entertainment, materialism, and pleasure, rather than seeking God's kingdom first.

- Jesus's return would be thought of as some vague, distant event by nearly all churchgoers with no real relevance to everyday life.

I'm sure you recognize the American Church in these bullet points. A church living in anticipation of the return of Jesus would look different. The conclusion is obvious: we are asleep. Jesus's words say so, and the characteristics of American churches support that conclusion.

JESUS'S TEACHING THAT WE ARE *ASLEEP* IS
REVOLUTIONARY *AND* FOUNDATIONAL.

WHAT DOES *ASLEEP* MEAN?

Scripture is inspired and interprets itself. So the Bible will define what Jesus meant by asleep. We don't have to guess.

> Therefore, be on the *alert*—for you do not know when the master of the house is coming, whether in the evening, at midnight, or when the rooster crows, or in the morning—in case he should come suddenly and find you *asleep*. What I say to you I say to all, "Be on the *alert!*" (Mark 13:35–37 NASB, emphasis mine)

> So then let us not *sleep* as others do, but let us be *alert* and sober. (1 Thessalonians 5:6 NASB, emphasis mine)

Notice that both of these passages show the opposite of being asleep is being alert or watchful. The conclusion of the parable of the ten virgins also shows that the parable is about being alert.

> Be on the *alert* then, for you do not know the day nor the hour
>
> (Matthew 25:13 NASB, emphasis mine)

When Jesus teaches that we are asleep, he means we are not being watchful or alert to the signs of his coming. If the Church is asleep, the events surrounding Jesus's return will take us by complete surprise.

Why Is the Church Asleep?

Does the parable of the ten virgins give insight into why the virgins (churchgoers) are sleeping? It does.

> But at midnight there was a shout, "Behold, the bridegroom! Come out to meet him." Then all those virgins rose and trimmed their lamps. (Matthew 25:6–7 NASB)

In order to understand these verses, we need to first understand the symbolism of the "shout" and the "lamps." Psalm 119:105 (NIV) tells us, "Your word is a lamp for my feet." From this we realize the meaning of *lamps* in this passage is God's Word. By extension, "trimmed their lamps" means searching the scriptures for answers. After the virgins hear the shout, the entire Church wakes up and hurries to check God's Word for what it says about our Savior's return.

We know the shout (a sign of his coming) is not the actual return of Jesus because the virgins have time to trim their lamps (check God's Word), and the foolish virgins then have more time to try and purchase oil for their lamps. *Oil* in this parable is the oil of anointing of the Holy Spirit that allows us to understand God's Word. Most likely, the symbolism of the shout in this parable is an earthshaking future event prior to Jesus's return. This event surprises the Church and wakes them up. Both wise and foolish churchgoers will then search scripture to understand what just happened.

This section of the parable gives us incredible insight into what is causing the virgins to sleep. The Church is asleep because it is holding mistaken views of what will occur prior to Jesus's return! How do we know this? We can be sure because after the wake-up call event, the virgins immediately trim their lamps—check out God's Word to see what it says about Jesus's return. If that earthshaking event had been consistent with their prior view of Jesus's return, it wouldn't have caused them to run to check their Bibles. They would have already understood what happened. Since they have to search the scriptures, we can be certain what is taking place in the world at that time will be a shock to them. We also know these mistaken views of Jesus's return are held by the vast majority of the Church because all ten virgins awaken, and *all ten* attempt to trim their lamps (search the scriptures).

Jesus's prophetic words have given us an amazing picture of what is to come. From just a handful of verses in Matthew 25, we have learned:

- The majority of the Church is asleep.

- The Church is sleeping because of mistaken views of what will happen prior to Jesus's return.

- A future event will occur that will awaken the Church to the reality that Jesus will return soon. This event will not be consistent with the view the majority of churchgoers hold today. Because of this they will search their Bibles for answers.

- Only those with *oil* (the Holy Spirit) for their lamps will be able to understand the scriptures.

I am sure you want to know what I believe these commonly held, mistaken views are. We will address them in later chapters. Right now let's return to the virgins. Unfortunately, the story does not have a happy ending for all of them. The foolish virgins do not have oil (the Holy Spirit) for their lamps and are unable to understand God's Word. They go in search of oil, but while they are searching, Jesus returns. He invites the wise virgins into the wedding feast and then shuts the door of heaven, leaving the foolish virgins in outer darkness. Jesus tells us why the foolish virgins were locked out.

> Those who were *ready* went in with him [Jesus] to the wedding feast; and the door was shut. Later the other virgins also came, saying, "Lord, Lord, open up for us." But he answered, "Truly I say to you, *I do not know you.*" (Matthew 25:10–12 NASB, emphasis and clarification mine)

Jesus doesn't say the foolish virgins don't know him or know about him. He said *he* doesn't know *them*. A personal relationship with Jesus is essential to having the Holy Spirit. There will be a wake-up call for the Church, but it will be too late for those who don't already have a relationship with Christ.

Also, notice Jesus uses the word "ready." He says that those who were ready went in with him. The Greek word translated "ready" is *hetoimos*, which means "to be prepared." We must be prepared for Jesus's return. We also must remain awake. We will discuss what *ready* means in later chapters. The modern Church assumes it means to have accepted Jesus as Savior. Of course, this is part of what being ready means. It is a prerequisite and the most important aspect, but there is much more.

Jesus's parable of the ten virgins suggests to us that half of current churchgoers will be shut out of his kingdom—as half of the virgins were foolish. This may not be a literal number, but even if it isn't, this is certainly a sober warning. There is great danger of being asleep in regard to Jesus's return.

Look around you this Sunday. Are some of those sitting near you in the pews foolish virgins? Are some of the churchgoers in your church at risk of having the door of heaven closed on them? These are serious questions. While we consider the answers, let me tell you a true story that further highlights the danger of being asleep in regard to Jesus's return.

A Thief in the Night

My head hit the pillow with a thud. It had been a long day; in fact, it had been three long, grueling days. The fellowship and teaching at the church conference I was attending were amazing, but twelve-hour schedules, the nervous emotions of my own public speaking, and a three-hour time difference from my home on the East Coast had drained all my remaining energy. I was ready for dreamland. While I usually have a hard time sleeping on the road, I thought, *not tonight*. I prayed an extremely short prayer of thanksgiving, as my eyes were already growing heavy.

Suddenly, I heard my door quietly unlock. As I struggled to open my eyes, I saw light streaming onto the floor. Someone was breaking into my hotel room!

"Hey, what are you doing?" I yelled. "Get out of here! Get out of my room."

Sounding shocked, a voice in a Middle Eastern accent mumbled, "Sorry, sorry." He backed out of my room and slammed the interior connecting door to the room next door.

I jumped out of bed, heart pounding, and sprinted to the connecting door. I had thrown the security latch on the front hallway door, but tired as I was, I had forgotten to bolt the interior connecting door as well. I peered through the peephole, but the thief was long gone. My heart still thumping, I relocked the connecting door and threw the security latch. Under my breath I mumbled to myself, "I'm in Las Vegas; why am I surprised?"

Here is the first piece of practical advice in this book: When you're in Las Vegas, always engage the security latch on hotel connecting doors! The danger was over, but I was spooked. What if I had been asleep? I lay back down on my bed saying a prayer of gratefulness that God had protected me. If I had fallen asleep, tired as I was, I might not have heard the thief and might not have woken up.

Then a peculiar, almost supernatural feeling came over me. Just that day I had taught on Jesus's illustration of the head of the house and the thief from Matthew 24. Later that night, I had lived it! God had allowed me to personally experience his Holy Word in the middle of the night in a Vegas hotel. God-moments like that happen occasionally and never without purpose.

In case you aren't familiar with it, here is the illustration of the head of the house and the thief from Matthew 24.

> But be sure of this, that if the head of the house had known at
> what time of the night the thief was coming, he would have
> been on the alert and would not have allowed his house to be

broken into. For this reason you also must be ready; for the
Son of Man is coming at an hour when you do not think He
will. (Matthew 24:43–44 NASB)

PERSECUTION, APOSTASY, AND DELIVERANCE

Before I explain the illustration, a brief understanding of the role of parables in the Olivet Discourse is in order. They do not occur in a vacuum; rather they exist in the greater context of Jesus's ninety-five verse sermon on events related to his return. Understanding the organization of this sermon as it appears in Matthew chapters 24 and 25 will assist us in a deeper appreciation of his related parables.

In Matthew 24:4–8, 31–35, Jesus gives us early warning signs that the end is about to begin. The rest of chapter 24 then gives three separate views of the period theologians call the great tribulation. We will discuss this period in more detail in chapter six: Eyes Wide Open. But for now, let's look at these three views of the same events which are shown from different perspectives. All three views discuss the main points Jesus wants to get across about this upcoming period of time.

- Believers will be persecuted;

- Many believers will fall away from the faith in what is called the great apostasy; and

- Jesus will return to deliver us and rule the world.

In Matthew 24:9–14, Jesus shows us how these factors will play out in the lives of believers. In Matthew 24:15–30, he prophesies major earthshaking events that will create the persecution, apostasy, and deliverance. Then in Matthew 24:42–51, he tells us two related parables about these same factors. The parables are told from the perspective of their effect on church leaders. In Matthew 25, Jesus adds three additional teachings, one of which is the parable of the ten virgins that we just studied. These three parables provide supplementary understanding about the three main points: persecution, apostasy, and deliverance. A graphic of the organization of Matthew 24 and how the verses of the chapter fit in the appropriate categories appears below:

Matt. 24	Signs	Persecution	Apostasy	Deliverance
vv. 4–8	vv. 4–8			
vv. 9–14		v. 9	vv. 10–13	v. 14
vv. 15–30	vv. 15, 27, 29	vv. 16–21	vv. 23–26	vv. 22, 28, 30
vv. 31–35	vv. 31–35			
vv. 36–41				vv. 36–41
vv. 42–51		v. 49	vv.42–45, 48–49	vv. 46–47, 50–51

Organization of Matthew 24

Some in the church teach that Matthew 24:9–14 relates to the first half of the tribulation period and Matthew 24:15–30 to the second half. This incorrect teaching falls apart on one word: therefore. One of the first rules you learn in Bible interpretation is that when you see *therefore* in a passage it's *there for* a reason. This is true in this context. Jesus connects the two passages (Matthew 24:9–14 and Matthew 24:15–30) with this word, which is the first word of verse 15, "Therefore when you see the ABOMINATION OF DESOLATION . . ." Jesus is telling his audience that when they see this terrible sign, all the events he just described in verses 9–14 are about to befall them.

Jesus also uses this same word, *therefore*, to set apart and delineate his third view of the great tribulation. In verse 42 he states, "Therefore be on the alert." In this section, Jesus tells two related parables that show the great tribulation from the perspective of church leaders.

I can't overstate how important a proper understanding of the context of Jesus's teaching is. If we don't understand the organization of Jesus's sermon, we will miss the critical teachings he is trying to get across to us.

And now that we have an understanding of context, we are ready to understand the illustration and how it relates to the break-in of my hotel room.

BREAKING AND ENTERING

The most intriguing character in the illustration is the thief. Who is the thief? Is it Jesus, as most in the Church traditionally teach? Jesus said he would return "like a thief in the night." Because of this statement, customary thinking equated Jesus's use of the word *thief* in Matthew 24:43 with the phrase "like a thief." That would seem to make sense, except the two uses of *thief* do not mean the same thing, and accepting the traditional interpretation will cause us to severely misinterpret what Jesus is trying to teach us.

Let's look at why Jesus cannot be the thief. As we do so, we must keep in mind the organization of the Olivet Discourse. This illustration and the parable that follows it are teaching about persecution, apostasy, and deliverance from the perspective of church leaders.

In the illustration, Jesus cannot be the thief primarily because in John's gospel, Jesus clearly tells us he *isn't* the thief.

> The thief comes only to steal and kill and destroy; I came that they may have life, and have it abundantly. (John 10:10 NASB)

Second, to make the nefarious meaning of the word *thief* clear, Jesus states in Matthew 24:43 that the thief breaks into the house. The Greek word translated "breaking in" is always associated with stealing or robbery in scripture. In Matthew 6, this same word is also used when Jesus advises us to lay up treasure in heaven where thieves cannot break in and steal. Stealing is not at all consistent with Jesus's nature. It's consistent with the nature of the true thief, who is Satan.

Third, the passage states that if the head of the house had been alert he would "not have allowed" his house to be broken into. This strongly implies the head of the house had the power to stop the thief. Jesus is all-powerful. If he were the thief, even if the head of the house was alert he would never be able to stop him.

Finally, Jesus cannot be the thief because he plays another role in the parable. Traditional Church interpretation has missed that the illustration of the head of the house and thief is really just the first portion of a longer parable, the parable of the faithful and the evil slaves. Notice that in the verse immediately following the illustration, the master chooses the head of his house. This shows continuation of the same thought.

> Who then is the faithful and sensible slave whom his master put in charge of his household to give them their food at the proper time? (Matthew 24:45 NASB)

For all these reasons, Jesus is the master, not the thief. Satan is the one who comes to "steal and kill and destroy." In the illustration of the head of the house and the thief, Jesus is beginning to expand on one of the main points about the great tribulation: apostasy.

"*LIKE* A THIEF IN THE NIGHT"

Before we continue the explanation of the illustration and fully accept that Satan is the thief, we must understand the phrase "like a thief" that Jesus uses about himself. These contradictory applications of the word *thief* are perplexing. Understanding what the phrase "like a thief in the night" meant in Jesus's day will put these contrasting uses of *thief* in perspective.

During the first century, this phrase was a Jewish idiom that meant something different than what we would normally believe it does today. Revelation refers to this idiom:

> Behold, I am coming as a thief. Blessed is he who watches, and keeps his garments, lest he walk naked and they see his shame. (Revelation 16:15 NKJV)

What does the phrase "like a thief" or "as a thief" mean? What's the connection with being naked? To twenty-first-century ears this is certainly odd. Understanding our Hebrew roots is essential here. During Jesus's day, when the Jewish temple was still standing, a priest was commanded to watch the fire on the altar by night so it would not go out. This was a holy fire, and it was essential that it stay lit. Priests took turns keeping watch. The captain of the guard patrolling the temple would come upon the priest unexpectedly, as a thief in the night. When the captain of the guard checked on his rounds, if a priest were found sleeping, the captain would take his torch and set the priest's garment on fire! The priest would be awakened by the fire and would run through the temple tearing off his burning clothing. This was quite an incentive to keep watch![2]

Do you see how perfectly this fits with Jesus's statement in Revelation 16 about keeping your garment and no one seeing your shame? The statement about a thief in the night refers to us being watchful for Jesus's return. We are to stay awake! Paul refers to this Jewish idiom as well.

> For you yourselves know full well that the day of the Lord will come just *like a thief in the night*. While they are saying, "Peace and safety!" then destruction will come upon them suddenly like labor pains upon a woman with child, and they will not escape. But you, brethren, are not in darkness, that the day would overtake you like a thief; for you are all sons of light and sons of day. We are not of night nor of darkness; so then *let us not sleep* as others do, but let us be *alert* and sober. (1 Thessalonians 5:2–6 NASB, emphasis mine)

> If any man's work is burned up, he will suffer loss; but himself will be saved, yet so *as through fire*. (1 Corinthians 3:15 NASB, emphasis mine)

"Like a thief in the night" is a figure of speech known as a simile. A simile compares two dissimilar items by demonstrating that they share a common trait. The temple guard was said to come like a thief because he approached the priest unexpectedly. He wasn't an actual thief and didn't break into or steal anything. When scripture says that Jesus comes like a thief, it implies he is coming unexpectedly to rapture his Church. The character in the illustration of the head of the house and the thief isn't said to be like a thief, he is the thief. And we know from Jesus's teachings the thief is coming to steal and kill and destroy.

THE MEANING OF THE ILLUSTRATION

In my opinion, this is the applicable interpretation: the heads of God's house on earth are church leaders, and the thief is Satan. It is the church leaders' responsibility to protect their house (their churches) from the thief. Unfortunately, the head of the house in the illustration experiences loss. The thief (Satan) breaks in, like the thief broke into my hotel room. Fortunately, I was awake and scared off the thief. The heads of God's house on earth, however, are mostly asleep. Now you can see why this event in my hotel room was a perfect picture of what Jesus is trying to teach us.

Did God put it into the mind of that thief to enter my room on the exact day I taught about this portion of God's Word? I think so. Was it a sign, at least for you and me? Yes, because it reinforces the understanding that if we are awake, we can protect our house from the thief, but if we are asleep, the thief will rob our house. Jesus is crystal clear on this point:

> *If* the head of the house had known at what time of the night the thief was coming, *he would have been on the alert* and would not have allowed his house to be broken into. (Matthew 24:43 NASB, emphasis mine)

There is the word *alert* again. It is the opposite of being asleep. If church leaders are awake, they can stop Satan from breaking into our churches. Now does the Bible teach about a time close to Jesus's return when Satan will steal souls from the Church? Yes, it is called the "great apostasy" or the "great falling away." (See 2 Thessalonians 2:3; Matthew 24:12–13.) We discuss this event in much more detail in chapter six: Eyes Wide Open. Apostasy is one of the three main points Jesus wants us to understand about the great tribulation, and I believe this short illustration describes that event. Can we know when this will occur? Jesus's own words say *if* the head of the house had watched, he could have prevented the break-in. If we stay awake and watch, we will know when the thief is coming.

The next verse states: "For this reason you also must be ready" (Matthew 24:44 NASB).

Jesus is telling us that we can prevent the thief from breaking into our churches, but we must be alert and prepared! Do you think our churches are preparing for this event? Are we preparing our families? Jesus is warning us, but unfortunately, our churches are asleep. Can you see how being asleep has led to the misinterpretation of this teaching—the mistaken view that Jesus is the thief—and how this misinterpretation has placed churchgoers in danger? The traditional Church interpretation gives the unprepared false comfort. If Jesus is the thief, the heads of the house (church leaders) can say to themselves, *We have prepared our congregations. We are ready because most have made a profession of faith.* If Satan is the thief, this illustration takes on a darker meaning. There is enormous risk because most congregations are not prepared to face him or his agents: the Antichrist and the False Prophet. A simple profession of faith by church-goers may not be enough. When discussing the great apostasy, Jesus states, "But the one who endures to the end, he will be saved" (Matthew 24:13 NASB). This implies more is involved than a simple profession of faith at the beginning; it requires enduring to the end.

JESUS'S ILLUSTRATIONS AND PARABLES
ARE WARNINGS THAT WE ARE IN DANGER.

THE HEAD OF THE HOUSE, THE THIEF, *AND* THE MASTER

We have already discussed how the illustration of the head of the house and thief, and the parable of the faithful and the evil slaves are really two parts of the same parable. In this expansive parable, Jesus further clarified who the head of the house is and how he is to act.

> Who then is the faithful and sensible slave whom his master put in charge of his household to give them their food at the proper time? Blessed is that slave whom his master finds so doing when he comes. Truly I say to you that he will put him in charge of all his possessions. But if that evil slave says in his heart, 'My master is not coming for a long time,' and begins to beat his fellow slaves and eat and drink with drunkards; the master of that slave will come on a day when he does not expect him and at an hour which he does not know, and will cut him in pieces and assign him a place with the hypocrites; in that place there will be weeping and gnashing of teeth. (Matthew 24:45–51 NASB)

We notice that the master has two slaves, one faithful and one evil. The Greek word translated "slave" is *doulos*, which means "one dedicated to the will of another." This word occurs an amazing 126 times in the New Testament, and nearly always refers to those who follow Jesus (churchgoers).

We will continue to examine this parable in both chapters six and seven in considerable detail. For now, we notice that the churchgoers Jesus places in charge of his household (church leaders) are both faithful and evil. Upon his return, Jesus will put the faithful church leaders in authority over all of his possessions, and he will cut the evil slave into pieces. In chapter six, we will learn the evil slave falls away in the great apostasy. We know this because the acts he commits in this parable are consistent with the great apostasy. We also notice this evil slave joins in the persecution of his brothers—he beats his fellow slaves. These verses reinforce the idea that this portion of scripture is about the three main features of the great tribulation—persecution, apostasy, and deliverance.

Those who believe discussing or preaching that the return of Jesus is irrelevant (or too controversial) miss this key point: the parables of Jesus teach that those within our own churches are in danger of being shut out of the kingdom of heaven. There is no excuse for us, as Jesus has told us: "Behold, I have told you in advance" (Matthew 24:25 NASB).

ARE YOU BEGINNING TO WAKE UP?

This chapter has been challenging. It has uncovered an aspect of Jesus's teaching about his return to which most have not been exposed. We learned that the majority of the Church is asleep, and one result of that slumber is being unable to properly interpret scripture. We saw this effect when we learned about the head of the house, the thief, and the master.

At this point you may be realizing that what we discussed in chapter one is true—if this book is correct, it might change your church and your life. Being asleep at this time in history is dangerous. Jesus has so many wonderful things for us to share in as we "prepare the way of the Lord." But we have to wake up. That is the purpose of this book. It was written to help the Church wake from its slumber to what the Holy Spirit wants us to know about preparing for Jesus's return.

> THE FIRST STEP TO WAKING UP IS TO
> ACKNOWLEDGE WE HAVE BEEN ASLEEP.

Clearing our minds of old, incorrect theories is easier said than done. Most of us cherish these old theories of Jesus's return; they are like a security blanket. I understand that completely. However, to wake up, I'm asking you to suspend your traditional ideas of Jesus's return until you finish this book. I am asking that you allow the Holy Spirit's instruction to overshadow what you have traditionally been taught. Our own personal cross which we take up daily may include humbling ourselves by laying down our closely held, traditional ideas of Jesus's return. When you complete the book, if you don't agree with what the scriptures within it say, you can always return to your current theory. An open mind to accurate biblical instruction, however, is critical to the working of the Holy Spirit.

TRADITIONAL THINKING

Traditions can be a wonderful thing. I am writing this section during the Hanukkah/Christmas season. Right now, I am looking at ornaments on our tree that my oldest daughter made for my wife and me twenty years ago. Those angels, created with macaroni and yarn, are priceless. When that same daughter was ten, she accidently melted wax on another, older ornament I had given my wife that says, *Our First Christmas Together*. I spent hours cleaning it.

Traditions can also be dangerous. Jesus warned us: "Neglecting the commandment of God, you hold to the tradition of men" (Mark 7:8 NASB). God's Word must be the arbiter of all our ideas, not historic teaching. Remember the Church is asleep, and sleeping saints developed many of the traditional theories we currently hold. These saints may have been mighty men of God, but in regard to Jesus's return, many were only dreaming.

We have learned how traditional thinking about the identity of the thief in Matthew 24:43 is mistaken. Ninety-nine percent of Christians hold the traditional view. Why are we now learning the truth about the thief's identity? We can't know for sure why God is choosing this time, but in general he seems to reveal just enough information for us to take the next step; not three steps; only the next step. "Without faith it is impossible to please him [God]" (Hebrews 11:6 NASB). If we understand everything about what is to transpire, we won't need faith. But now, perhaps, a little more of God's plan has been revealed because it's time for all of us to take the next step.

If you hate the thought of giving up traditional ideas of Christ's return as much as the thought of giving up an ornament labeled *Our First Christmas Together*, let's take a brief look at two other scriptures that discuss God withholding understanding about his Word. God's Word is eternal and unchanging, but our understanding of it may change.

> But as for you, Daniel, conceal these words and seal up the book until the end of time; many will go back and forth, and knowledge will increase. (Daniel 12:4 NASB)

Did you know that God personally commanded the book of Daniel to be sealed until end of time? Might sealing the understanding of a book of the Bible on which so much of other prophecy is based confuse our thinking? Notice the verse also says that many will go back and forth (throughout other books of the Bible to learn more) and that eventually knowledge (of prophecy) will increase. I am sure that increase in knowledge will be incremental, though—only enough for us to take the next step.

> And the disciples came and said to Him, "Why do You speak to them in parables?" Jesus answered them, "To you it has been granted to know the mysteries of the kingdom of heaven, but to them it has not been granted. For whoever has, to him more shall be given, and he will have an abundance; but whoever does not have, even what he has shall be taken away from him. Therefore I speak to them in parables; because while seeing they do not see, and while hearing they do not hear, nor do they understand. (Matthew 13:10–13 NASB)

Jesus quotes this passage later in the Olivet Discourse. Notice how he grants understanding of parables to some and denies the understanding to others. We must all hold our traditional theories of Jesus's return loosely in fear and awe. God's ways are not our ways.

Before we leave chapter two, let's pray, asking for the Holy Spirit's guidance and for him to be our teacher:

> Spirit of the Living God fall *fresh* on us all. Help us wake up, but wake us gently. We realize in regard to events as intimate as your return, great emotion has already been invested. Please help us see that what you have planned for us is more wonderful, more exciting, and more amazing than anything we have conceived on our own. Cause those things in this book that are truly of you to reverberate within our souls. Cause them to *glow* with your holy glory! Help us to know that instinctively they are true. Also cause those things that we have invented out of our humanness to be forgotten and blow away like chaff. Help us all, Lord, to come to a deeper knowledge of you and your will for us, and help us to want that will for our lives. Amen and Amen.

SUMMARY

This second chapter presents the most foundational point we need to understand about Jesus's return. The vast majority of the Church is asleep and unwatchful. The cause of this sleepiness is a mistaken understanding of what will occur prior to that glorious day. Because of this, we need to suspend all our pet theories of Jesus's return and allow the Holy Spirit to help us awaken and prepare for what is to come.

The basic steps for getting ready for Jesus from this chapter are:

1. **The Church is asleep:**
   We need to wake up ourselves and then help awaken the Church.

2. **Traditional ideas about Jesus's return may be inaccurate:**
   We need to reevaluate them.

3. **The thief is coming:**
   The risk to the Church is high. We need to watch and get ready.

In the next chapter, we will discuss how to recognize and then utilize the treasure we've been given in order to prepare for Jesus's return.

So, rise and shine.

CHAPTER THREE

MONOPOLY MONEY:

HOW TO RECOGNIZE OUR TREASURE

For to those who have, more will be given, and they will have an abundance; but from those who have nothing, even what they have will be taken away. (Matthew 13:12 NRSV)

Monopoly is one of the most popular board games in the world. There are hundreds of versions, Dog-Opoly (where the properties are all dog breeds), Duke-Opoly for fans of Duke University, Batman-Opoly for superhero fans, and even Anti-Monopoly where the goal is to be the first to go bankrupt. Everyone has a favorite playing piece. Mine is the top hat. You may also have met players who fulfill this scripture: "To those who have, more will be given." It seems like those players can't lose. Every trade of property they make seems to work out in their favor. Even if they trade away Boardwalk for a lesser property, they still win.

Jesus explained that same principle in the parable of the talents. It teaches about what is valuable and how we are to invest what we've been given. It's found in the Olivet Discourse, and just like the parable of the ten virgins, and the illustration of the head of the house and the thief, it is a parable that specifically teaches about how to prepare for Jesus's return.

I remember hearing the parable of the talents from my earliest days as a Christian. At that time, I was taught a more general application. We usually hear the parable means God has given us talents and abilities, and we are to develop them for his kingdom purposes. This is a perfectly fine application, but it doesn't really hit the bull's-eye of what I think Jesus had in mind for us. Let's look at the opening verses:

> For it is just like a man about to go on a journey, who called his own slaves and entrusted his possessions to them. To one he gave five talents, to another, two, and to another, one, each according to his own ability; and he went on his journey. (Matthew 25:14 –15 NASB)

As we begin to study the parable, we notice that it's a further explanation of the principles of the previous parable of the ten virgins in Matthew 25:1–12. In the parable of the talents, the master is going on a long journey and entrusts his property consisting of talents to his slaves. The word translated *talent* is the key to understanding the parable. In our English vernacular, this word has a meaning of "ability or giftedness." However, the etymology of our English word *talent* comes from a meaning of wealth— that our abilities and giftedness are a form of wealth. The etymology can be traced back to the Greek word used in this passage: *talanton*, which means "a weight or measure."[3] Specifically, it was slang for a measure of gold or silver that weighed a talent. The value of a talent of gold in 2015 is $840,000. A talent of silver is worth $10,800.

Regardless of which weight or measure Jesus referred to, it is a large sum of money. Especially if Jesus was referring to gold talents, it was an incredibly large amount of money—a fortune. Jesus was exaggerating for effect. He was saying that these talents given to the slaves by their master were worth more than any earthly treasure most of us will see in our lifetimes.

What does this parable mean? Jesus wasn't recommending that we place our money in the bank and earn as much interest as possible. He wants us to utilize what we've been given, not to horde it. It is not a parable about investing money. But it is a parable about what is valuable.

ADVANCE TOKEN TO BOARDWALK

Do you ever wish it was as easy to earn a living as it appears to be in the game Monopoly? I do. Another player draws the card "Advance token to Illinois Avenue." They pick up their playing piece and set it down on your property. They pay you the rent, and instantly you are $26 richer.

As you become engrossed in the game, it's easy to believe the Monopoly money has value. Within the game it does. You can pay your debts and buy houses. But take that $26 Monopoly money you earned from the rent payment and try to buy a loaf of bread at the local grocery store. They might call their security guard or the local psychiatric hospital. We quickly learn Monopoly money has value only within the game.

When I open my wallet and look at the ones, fives, and occasional twenty, I try to think about them the same way. I consider US dollars to be Monopoly money. They only have value within this game we call the world. US dollars have no eternal value in and of themselves (although we act like they do). They can be utilized for many worthwhile and eternal purposes, but wealth and materialism alone have no eternal value.

THE RUG

America sits on a comfortable financial rug right now. We are one of the most blessed nations in history, and have been given a lot of Monopoly money. That blessing has made us complacent and has lulled us to sleep. I would not be surprised to see God pull the rug out from under us. If you are reading this and feeling that you don't want to get off the rug that you are snuggled up on right at this moment, consider that God may have a plan for your life that doesn't involve the rug. That plan may seem harsh to you, but the blessing he has planned for you far outweighs the temporary comfort you may lose.

"And we know that God causes all things to work together for good to those who love God, to those who are called according to His purpose" (Romans 8:28 NASB). That includes pruning us from those things that prevent us from being fruitful, as John stated in his gospel: "Every branch that bears fruit, He prunes it so that it may bear more fruit" (John 15:2 NASB).

I believe all of us in America need to prepare to be pruned. I have already begun to imagine my life without my comfortable financial rug. I recommend you do as well. I have been saving and paying off bills in anticipation of what may come. I have also begun to live under my means, cutting expenses back to only those things that are necessary. The interesting result of this self-imposed financial pruning is that I have come to value materialistic things less and spiritual things more. Pruning may seem harsh, but it may free us to wake up and live for Christ's kingdom rather than for ourselves.

Scientific economic theories support the idea that Americans will be pruned. One of the most prominent economic cycle theories is known as the "Kondratiev wave," which was developed by a Russian economist named Nikolai Kondratiev. Kondratiev theorized that all economies move in cycles of expansion, boom, recession, and depression. Professor W. Thompson of Indiana University has done analysis of the Kondratiev wave theory. His analysis shows America is headed into a severe economic depression that should last until the year 2020.[4]

Many other similar economic-cycle theories also seem to indicate that economic trouble is ahead for the United States. These include Charles Nenner research, the Kress cycles, the Elliott wave, the market energy waves, the Armstrong economics, and cycles per Charles Hugh Smith. Without going into specific detail, all of these sources point to a worldwide economic crash or correction during the period 2015–2020.[5]

If we imagine this American life and lifestyle remaining constant, we are fooling ourselves. Our typical American preoccupation with affluence may be about to come to a screeching halt. All of us need to be about our Master's business. Money does not have the value we ascribe to it. Many of us are about to learn that lesson the hard way.

TIME

How we spend our time says a great deal about what we value. In our lives we amuse ourselves with myriad good things: sports, education, vacations, etc. Of themselves, these things are not evil. But those things that are not applied to furthering the kingdom won't last; they are not eternal. I was interested to learn that the English word "amuse" comes from two separate Old French words: "a" meaning "opposite" or "against," and "muse" meaning "to think." Our amusements are against thinking and are causing us to sleep as well.

Our amusements won't last because Jesus is coming like a thief in the night. He is like the guard making rounds in the temple and is going to burn up our amusements with his torch. We may be saved, but as through fire. If you think you don't have time to awaken the Church, consider reprioritizing. Those things that are eternal will not burn, but our amusements will. If we have chosen not to reprioritize our lives, we may still be saved in Jesus, but we will wish we had sought his kingdom first.

> If any man's work is burned up, he will suffer loss; but he himself will be saved, yet so *as through fire*. (1 Corinthians 3:15 NASB, emphasis mine)

SHARE WHAT YOU'VE LEARNED

If Jesus wasn't alluding to money or to abilities, what is the parable of the talents really about? In my opinion, Proverbs 8:10 (NIV) holds the key: "Choose my instruction instead of silver, knowledge rather than choice gold." What property has the master entrusted to his slaves? That which is worth more than choice gold: his gospel. This is consistent with the testimony of God's Word. The gospel is our treasure and power:

> For I am not ashamed of the gospel, for it is the power of God for salvation to everyone who believes, to the Jew first and also to the Greek. (Romans 1:16 NASB)

OUR TREASURE IS THE GOSPEL.

In this parable of the talents we see that the master distributes his treasure to his slaves. He dispenses it based on the varying abilities of his workers, so ability and giftedness do play a role in the parable, but they are not the treasure. They are the factors the master uses to decide how much treasure to initially give each of his workers. We then observe how the slaves utilize what they have been given.

> Immediately the one who had received the five talents went and traded with them, and gained five more talents. In the same manner the one who had received the two talents gained two more. But he who received the one talent went away, and dug a hole in the ground and hid his master's money. (Matthew 25:16–18 NASB)

The slave that received the five talents traded them to produce another five talents. What a unique thought if the talent is truly the gospel. The slave trades, or does business, with the knowledge of scripture he has been given, and receives greater knowledge. How many times have my brothers in Christ called me or e-mailed me to discuss a portion of God's Word and we both came away the richer? How many times have I taught or written on the gospel only to learn what I never would have otherwise? If we do business with God's Word, we increase our own knowledge in addition to having an impact on others.

This parable in Matthew 25 is the perfect follow-up to the parable of the ten virgins. Not only do we need oil (the Holy Spirit) to light our lamps so we can understand God's Word, we need to trade or do business with the scriptures. We are to share what we've been given.

A second meaning also seems obvious. By trading scriptures, the kingdom expands and faith increases. Sharing God's Word *is* our Master's business, and we need to prepare for Jesus's return by being active in his business.

A HOLE IN THE GROUND

Jesus also shows us what we are *not* to do with our knowledge of the gospel. The slave with one talent buries it. None of us wants to be that slave. But before we smugly assume that we are following Jesus's command, let us carefully examine what this treasure, the gospel, truly is.

Context is always important in understanding any portion of scripture. As mentioned previously, the parable of the talents is found within the Olivet Discourse. Because it's found in this portion of scripture that deals with Jesus's return, its meaning is directly linked to it. By extension, the gospel is also linked to it.

If you ask a Christian today what the gospel is, you will hear that it's the good news. It is! You will also probably hear that the gospel is that Christ died for our sins and rose from the dead. Hallelujah! This truly is good news. But what does God's Word say? Paul discussed the gospel in these verses:

> Now I make known to you, brethren, the gospel which I preached to you, which also you received, in which also you stand, by which also you are saved, if you hold fast the word which I preached to you, unless you believed in vain. For I delivered to you as of first importance what I also received, that Christ died for our sins according to the scriptures, and that He was buried, and that He was raised on the third day according to the scriptures. (1 Corinthians 15:1–4 NASB)

Most Christians assume that this is a complete synopsis of the gospel and stop reading right there. But it is only the first half of the gospel. Paul continues throughout this chapter of 1 Corinthians 15 to explain how the first half of the gospel is linked to the second half.

Now I say this, brethren, that flesh and blood cannot inherit the kingdom of God; nor does the perishable inherit the imperishable. Behold, I tell you a mystery; we will not all sleep, but we will all be changed, in a moment, in the twinkling of an eye, at the last trumpet; for the trumpet will sound, and the dead will be raised imperishable, and we will be changed. (1 Corinthians 15:50–52 NASB)

THE GOSPEL INCLUDES THE FIRST COMING AND THE SECOND COMING OF JESUS.

One without the other is not the complete gospel. Yet, in many of our churches, Jesus's return has become a taboo subject, and church leaders often find it difficult to share what they know. By not doing business with the scriptures about the second coming, their flock is left defenseless, and the leader himself does not grow.

Ignoring the complete gospel has become commonplace in the Church. Pastor Rick Warren is the author of *The Purpose Driven Life* (Zondervan, 2002). This book has sold over thirty million copies and spent years on the *New York Times* best-seller list. Many refer to him as America's foremost spiritual advisor.[6] Yet on page 285 of this million-selling book he makes this outrageous statement:

When the disciples wanted to talk about prophecy, Jesus quickly switched the conversation to evangelism. He wanted them to concentrate on their mission in the world. He said in essence, "The details of my return are none of your business. What is your business is the mission I have given you."

Pastor Warren was referring to Acts 1:6–8, where Jesus instructs his disciples that they cannot know the precise timing of his return. There are no verses in scripture that instruct us not to pay attention to the details of Christ's return. In fact, forty-five days prior to speaking the words in Acts 1:6–8, Jesus had given the disciples the most extensive explanation of his return in the entire Bible. In Matthew alone, that explanation comprises a sermon of ninety-five verses. It is one of the longest unbroken quotes of Jesus in all of scripture. We know it as the Olivet Discourse.

Hopefully, many of this nation's pastors who share Pastor Warren's dangerous view of scripture will have a chance to reevaluate their position. The consequences of their current thinking are horrific for their flock and for themselves. In the parable of the talents, the master's response to burying our knowledge of his complete gospel was particularly harsh.

> You wicked, lazy slave, you knew that I reap where I did not sow and gather where I scattered no seed. Then you ought to have put my money in the bank, and on my arrival I would have received my money back with interest. Therefore take away the talent from him, and give it to the one who has the ten talents. For to everyone who has, more shall be given, and he will have an abundance; but from the one who does not have, even what he does have shall be taken away. Throw out the worthless slave into the outer darkness; in that place there will be weeping and gnashing of teeth. (Matthew 25:26–30 NASB)

This is a difficult teaching. Jesus's own words tell us that we will be judged on how we handle his complete gospel, including his first coming and his second coming. Many in our churches are preparing for Jesus's return by preaching what they think is the gospel. By this they mean preaching about Jesus's first coming. The salvation Jesus paid for on the cross is essential. Unfortunately it is only the first half of the gospel.

Jesus has a heart for the lost. As a Church we have shared in his passion for his first coming; we need to acquire that passion for the second coming as well and present the complete gospel.

SEEING THEY DO NOT SEE

Jesus ends the parable of the talents by quoting from Matthew 13, where he explains to us why he teaches in parables.

> And the disciples came and said to Him, "Why do You speak to them in parables?" Jesus answered them, "To you it has been granted to know the mysteries of the kingdom of heaven, but to them it has not been granted. For whoever has, to him more shall be given, and he will have an abundance; but whoever does not have, even what he has shall be taken away from him. Therefore I speak to them in parables; because while seeing they do not see, and while hearing they do not hear, nor do they understand." (Matthew 13:10–13 NASB)

This quoted passage clearly shows the parable of the talents is about sharing the knowledge of God, making clear what is hidden in scripture. It is also apparent that prophecy about Jesus's return is akin to parables and is given in a veiled form so the wise understand and the foolish do not. Are some of our teachers among the ones Jesus refers to as "while seeing they do not see . . . nor do they understand" (Matthew 13:13 NASB)?

Let us be about our Master's business; let us trade scriptures with one another. Feel free to utilize this book in your teaching, and preach the gospel in and out of season. As we do business with the wealth God has given us in his gospel, we ourselves will become richer in our knowledge just as the player in a Monopoly game becomes richer as he shrewdly trades properties to establish a monopoly.

ADVANCE TO GO: COLLECT $200

Interestingly, there is even more to this parable. Jesus tells the faithful slaves who have doubled their wealth that they will rule cities. Somehow I don't believe this aspect of the parable is symbolic as to the reward. I think Jesus meant exactly what he said. Those who have proven faithful in little (the sharing of his complete gospel) have received training for their next assignment—managing cities in God's coming millennial kingdom on earth. That is a fascinating concept!

What happens to the slave that hides the gospel of Jesus's first and second coming? Jesus tells us that the little he has been given is taken away, and he is cast into outer darkness. This seems unusually severe punishment for simply not preaching about Jesus's return. It is consistent, however, with the other parables at the end of the Olivet Discourse. In the illustration of the head of the house and the thief, the head of the house allows his house to be broken into. In the parable of the faithful and evil slaves (see chapter seven: Sibling Rivalry), the evil slave is cut into pieces. In the parable of the ten virgins, the foolish virgins are locked out of the kingdom. Serious punishment!

Slaves and virgins are both terms that are appropriately used for churchgoers, yet in these parables they find themselves eternally separated from God. How can that be? In the last chapter, we learned that an event is coming called the "the great falling away" or "the great apostasy." Is it possible that these churchgoers fall away from the faith at that time? We will show how this is exactly what happens to them in chapter six: Eyes Wide Open. At this time, however, let's look at the characteristics of each of these churchgoers that cause them to fall away.

Parable	Churchgoer	Reason for falling away
Head of the house and the thief (Matt. 24:42–44)	Head of the house	Not alert, not watchful
Faithful and evil slaves (Matt. 24:45–51)	Evil slave	Thought his master's coming was a long way off
Ten virgins (Matt. 25:1–13)	Foolish virgin	No oil (Holy Spirit) for her lamp
Talents (Matt. 25:14–30)	Worthless slave	Hid the gospel of the first and second coming due to fear

Churchgoers Who Fall Away

All of the reasons for falling away are consistent with being asleep. Specifically, in the case of the worthless slave who doesn't preach the second coming, he avoids doing business with his talent because he's afraid. Perhaps he feels his church will not accept the message. If a churchgoer is afraid to share the second coming in our current safe environment, isn't it likely that he will be even more afraid to acknowledge Christ when his faith is tested during the great apostasy?

SUMMARY

In this chapter three, we learned that our true treasure is the gospel and not our financial resources. As we saw in chapter two, Jesus has again shown us that churches are at risk. In this chapter, we saw that the risk was not utilizing the complete gospel, which is the first and second coming of Christ.

What will be our response? Will we continue to accumulate our Monopoly money (US dollars) as if it has lasting worth? Will we continue to preach half a gospel, or will we place our value on the complete gospel and work to awaken the Church?

In the next chapter, we will begin to examine what our attitude needs to be in order to properly prepare for Christ's return.

The basic steps for getting ready for Jesus from this chapter are:

> 1. **It is likely our affluent way of life will end:**
>   **We need to transform our values around what really matters.**
> 2. **The gospel is both the first and second comings of Christ:**
>   **We need to preach the complete gospel.**

In the next chapter we will begin to examine what our attitude needs to be in order to properly prepare for Christ's return.

CHAPTER FOUR

IT'S A WEDDING!

HOW TO ADJUST OUR ATTITUDE

Jesus spoke to them again in parables, saying, "The kingdom of heaven may be compared to a king who gave a wedding feast for his son. And he sent out his slaves to call those who had been invited to the wedding feast." (Matthew 22:1–3 NASB)

My wife had a most unusual plan for our wedding reception: hula hoops. After we arrived at the reception, she brought out four hula hoops, one each for my dad, her dad, my best man, and one for me. She then invited the four of us to embarrass ourselves by having a hula hoop contest. Not one of us was able to keep his hoop spinning for more than ten seconds! It was hilarious—mass incoordination.

Jesus tells us his return will be a wedding and that a reception known as the Wedding Feast of the Lamb (Wedding Supper of the Lamb—NIV) is coming. The reception probably won't feature hula hoops (but, who knows? Jesus has a great sense of humor), but it is not one any of us should plan to miss.

Who are going to be the bride and groom at this wedding? Jesus is the bridegroom, and his Church is going to be the bride! Scripture tells us the relationship of Christ to his bride is a great mystery.

For this reason a man shall leave his father and mother and shall be joined to his wife, and the two shall become one flesh. This *mystery* is great; but I am speaking with reference to Christ and the church. (Ephesians 5:31–32 NASB, emphasis mine)

Knowing that Jesus's return is like a wedding is critical to getting ready. We don't prepare for a wedding the same way we prepare for a soccer game. There are four aspects of this wedding we need to highlight in our minds in order to prepare our attitude so we are ready.

- It is a time to rejoice!

- We need to send out invitations.

- The period before the wedding is chaotic.

- We need to remain pure for our bridegroom.

REJOICE, AND AGAIN I SAY REJOICE!

When our popular Christian culture discusses Jesus's return, it seems to emphasize the doom and gloom aspects of judgment. This is because most people are asleep to reality. The unsaved may view Jesus's return that way, but if we place his return in proper perspective, it will be wonderful beyond imagination for those of us who have saving faith in Christ. We may face difficult times, but we do not need to be frightened about Jesus's return. Scripture calls it our blessed hope, not our blessed fear. Perfect love drives out all fear, and that is what Jesus wants for us. God desires to comfort his people. It is Satan who wants to scare us. (Peter calls him a roaring lion.) Rather than being fearful, we need to get excited about Jesus's wedding. It will be the most important event in history! We need to have a proper perspective.

ADJUST YOUR ATTITUDE AND REJOICE!

When my wife said "yes" and we became engaged, I was overjoyed as never before in my life. God had given me this wonderful woman to be my life partner. I couldn't wait to marry her and wanted the whole world to know. You and I are in an engagement period right now with Jesus. We are not yet married; this is not as good as it gets. It will get much, much better, so we should have an anticipatory feeling about his return.

The Church has lost this rush of joy as a result of our being asleep. It is hard to anticipate when you are in dreamland. If a church is not preaching Jesus's return on a regular basis and doesn't proclaim it as our blessed hope, then how can they say they are looking forward to it?

When I was engaged to my wife, I couldn't stop talking about her. Now, this isn't to say that our engagement period didn't have its share of difficulties. We lived in two different states. (Jesus and the Church also live in different "states," heaven and earth, but soon we will be joined together just as my wife and I were.) Living in different states meant long periods apart from one another and resulted in a deep longing. The trips to visit were difficult and somewhat dangerous in winter. But because of the joy of what was to come, we easily and happily endured it. The Bible says of Jesus: "Who for the joy set before Him endured the cross" (Hebrews 12:2 NASB).

Jesus's joy was being united with us! He endured the cross just for that joy. We must never forget that. Jesus calls all of us to take up our own cross and follow him. This does mean sacrificing and giving up earthly comforts, but it doesn't mean giving up our joy. Will we face difficulties before Jesus returns? Yes. Will Jesus be with us and help us? Even more assuredly, YES! He has promised, "Lo, I am with you always, even to the end of the age" (Matthew 28:20 NASB).

Why should we endure? Because of the joy Christ is setting before us. In fact, scripture calls it a privilege to suffer for Christ.

> For he has graciously granted you the *privilege* not only of believing in Christ, but of *suffering for him* as well. (Philippians 1:29 NRSV, emphasis mine)

A concept like this is only discerned spiritually. If we are thinking with our flesh, we obviously can't understand how it can be a privilege to suffer for Christ. As my wife and I look back upon our engagement to each other, we look back on the difficulties with joy. They are among our most cherished memories. After Christ returns, I am sure we will celebrate the difficulties we endured for him. Christ would never deny us the cherished memories of what we will have endured for him during our engagement.

A friend mentioned to me that her father commented on facing difficulties prior to Jesus's return by saying, "My Jesus would never do that to me." I think this statement should be turned upside down: My Jesus would never deny us the privilege of remembering our sacrifices for him through all eternity.

I imagine a night not too far in the future. We are all sitting around the fire in Jesus's kingdom telling stories. Jesus says, "Nelson (or Mike or Suzy [insert your name here]), one of my fondest memories is when you . . ." Then Jesus himself, the king of the universe, proceeds to tell all of us what you endured to show him you loved him. I cannot imagine my Jesus ever denying us that moment.

If we are unwilling to endure for Jesus, we must ask ourselves, is it really love? We should let that sink in. If I weren't willing to endure difficult travel and getting up at three a.m. to visit my fiancée, what would her opinion have been of my commitment? What would my wife-to-be have thought if I wouldn't travel to see her and, instead, made her make all the sacrifices?

Jesus's nail-scarred hands will be a reminder of what he endured for us. He made the ultimate sacrifice. To think our relationship to Jesus should be all take and no give, however, is nonsense. Our memories of suffering will be reminders of what we endured for him and will be proof to us of our love for him throughout all eternity. Our relationship to Jesus is a forever love story and outshines all human love stories.

THE TIME PRIOR TO JESUS'S RETURN

SHOULD BE JOYFUL.

When it comes to Jesus's return, we are to rejoice! Our bridegroom is coming! Pray that God will grant you this joyful spirit even in the midst of persecution. It is essential if you are going to accomplish what he desires of you.

WEDDING INVITATIONS

Last year, our eldest daughter was married to a wonderful man. She was the kind of child who dreamed about weddings from her earliest years. She performed literally hundreds of stuffed animal weddings at our house while she was growing up. When it was time for her to plan her own wedding, she had very specific ideas about what she wanted. Unfortunately, her dad is not a wealthy man. She had to choose between a fancy but small wedding opposed to a larger wedding but less elaborate reception. She chose fancy, and it was difficult for her to leave friends and relatives off the invitation list.

Fortunately, our heavenly Father is sparing no expense for the spiritual wedding of his Son, Jesus, that is approaching. We can invite as many friends and relatives as we want. In fact, the more invitations we send out, the happier our Father will be! God's heart has always been about salvation. The Father wants everyone to attend the wedding of his Son.

> The Lord is not slow about His promise [to return], as some count slowness, but is patient toward you, *not wishing for any to perish* but for all to come to repentance. But the day of the Lord will come like a thief. (2 Peter 3:9–10 NASB, clarification mine)

OUR PRIVILEGE: INVITING AS MANY AS POSSIBLE TO GOD'S WEDDING FEAST.

God wants all of us to come to repentance, and everyone to have saving faith in his Son. Therefore, he wants the gospel proclaimed in the entire world.

> This gospel of the kingdom shall be preached in the whole world as a testimony to all the nations, *and then the end will come.* (Matthew 24:14 NASB, emphasis mine)

Wow! Do you see that? The gospel must be preached to the whole world before Jesus will return. In his second letter, Peter tells us that we can even hasten the day.

> What sort of people ought you to be in holy conduct and godliness, looking for *and hastening* the coming of the day of God? (2 Peter 3:11–12 NASB, emphasis mine)

How can we hasten the day of Jesus's return? Possibly, one way is by proclaiming the gospel to those who haven't heard it. In Matthew 24:14, the word translated "the nations" is the Greek word *ethnos*, which means "people groups." Estimates of how many ethnos exist vary widely. The estimates range from 10,000 to 27,000. If an ethnos is defined by a common ethnic background and language, there are 13,000 such groups.[7] Of these groups, approximately 40 percent are classified as unreached (no knowledge of the gospel) or least-reached groups (limited knowledge of the gospel). Two billion people live in these groups, and twenty-six million die each year without scriptural knowledge of our Savior.[8]

The majority of the unreached people groups are in what is termed the "10/40 Window."

This is a section of world located between ten and forty degrees north of the equator that contains the Muslim realm, the Hindus of India, and the Buddhists and atheists of China. When we think about the 10/40 Window, we naturally think about overseas missions, but many of those

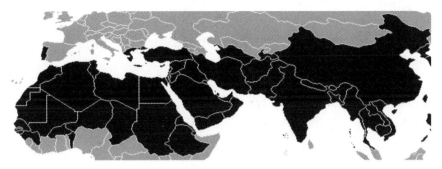

The 10/40 Window

people groups live right here in the USA. Reaching out to these groups is a priority, and many live right in our hometowns. Reaching these groups involves overseas missions and hometown missions.

OUTREACH, NOT OUTRAGE

You have seen the headlines: "Islamic Terrorists Gun Down Cartoonists"; "Millions Hit the Streets of Paris in Protest"; "Factory Worker in Oklahoma Beheads a Coworker", and the nation is outraged. Jesus's words in the Olivet Discourse are beginning to ring true:

> Because of the increase of wickedness, the love of *most* will grow cold. (Matthew 24:12 NIV, emphasis mine)

But this verse is not about what many think it is. I used to believe this verse referred to unbelievers. Now I'm beginning to believe it's *my* love that is growing cold. Maybe it's all our love that is growing cold as well.

When you see a terrorist act, what is your gut level, emotional response: anger, hatred, and fear? How many feel sorrow for the terrorist who died without Jesus?

American media has been busy spinning news stories with the intention of dividing us and increasing our hatred and fear of one another. And like sheep, we are being led astray. Many hate the Muslims we should be witnessing to; and Satan is laughing. We are allowing the wickedness of terrorists to cause our love to grow cold. We are rightly hating the wickedness but forgetting our great commission. We are thinking like Americans, not Christ followers.

On September 11, 2001, radical Islamists from the 10/40 Window drove planes into the Twin Towers in NYC, and the Pentagon in Washington, DC. If not for the valiant efforts of the passengers of United Flight 93, they would have crashed into the White House. In response, the United States spent six trillion dollars[9] on wars in Afghanistan and Iraq. It is estimated that nearly a million soldiers served in these wars at one time or another.[10]

This is not a political statement, but what if the United States had spent trillions of dollars sending a million missionaries to the 10/40 Window instead? What might have been the result of such spiritual warfare? After all, our struggle is not against the flesh and blood power of Islam, but it is against the evil one and his demons.

> For our struggle is not against flesh and blood, but against the rulers, against the powers, against the world forces of this darkness, against the spiritual forces of wickedness in the heavenly places. (Ephesians 6:12 NASB)

This missionary army could have sent two hundred missionaries to each and every unreached people group in the world! Admitting the challenges with languages and untranslated scripture, might the Great Commission (Matthew 28:19–20) have already been fulfilled?

When I see terrorist acts, one of the first things that comes to my mind, beyond the tragedy, is that it might have been prevented by a missionary. If the terrorist had heard the gospel, they *might* have repented and become a Christian. The only way to overcome the evil of Islam is through the good of the gospel.

The initial reaction of Christians to sending their sons and daughters into the 10/40 Window might be safety concerns. It's interesting that we are willing to send our children as soldiers to this area, and deem debilitating injury and death as acceptable sacrifices, but we resist sending missionaries. Those of us who are Christians seem always to focus on defending ourselves against evil. It is important to ask God for protection, but I believe he would prefer we take the offense against Satan and his empire. Look at this verse: "Upon this rock I will build My church; and the gates of Hades will not overpower it" (Matthew 16:18 NASB).

Most of us are familiar with this passage, but please notice something. Jesus was referring to the *gates* of Hades. Gates are not used for offense; they are defensive structures. God is saying Satan's defenses will not prevail against us. The Church's offense will overcome them. Here is another fascinating verse:

> The accuser of our brethren [Satan] has been thrown down, he who accuses them before our God day and night. And they overcame him because of the blood of the Lamb and because of the word of their testimony, and they did not love their life even when faced with death. (Revelation 12:10–11 NASB, clarification mine)

This passage teaches us that we will overcome Satan by the blood of the Lamb, by our testimony, and our willingness to face hard times, even life-threatening situations. Doesn't this perfectly describe sending missionaries to the 10/40 Window? The way of victory is always difficult. Jesus's victory came on a cross, and his was the ultimate sacrifice. In a similar manner, he asked us to take up our own cross and follow him. We overcome evil with good. Many are rightly troubled by radical Islam, overseas and at home. But the route to victory is the same—it's the cross.

GOD DESIRES WE TAKE THE OFFENSE AGAINST
SATAN, NOT JUST BE ON THE DEFENSE.

The way may seem difficult, but the eternal rewards from God are great. God is throwing a huge wedding reception. He wants everyone there. He wants us to invite as many people as possible. And we have assurance that he will be with us. The difficulty of taking up our cross and following Jesus is an illusion. It is actually the most rewarding thing we can possibly do. It is also the safest place we can possibly be because that is where he will be. The rewards of the world are nothing compared to following Jesus.

A SPECIAL FORM OF EVANGELISM

I would like to make another point about evangelism. There will be a special form of evangelism available to us prior to Jesus's return. It is called apocalyptic evangelism. The best way to describe it is to give an example from the Bible. In Acts 2, Peter delivered the first sermon of the Church on the day of Pentecost. The 120 believers who had stayed true to Jesus were in the upper room when the Holy Spirit came upon them. They began speaking the praises of God in foreign languages, and thousands gathered to hear and see this great thing. Some accused them of drunkenness. In reply, Peter quoted the Old Testament prophet Joel:

> But this is what was spoken of through the prophet Joel: "And it shall be in the last days," God says, "That I will pour forth of My Spirit on all mankind; and your sons and your daughters shall prophesy, and your young men shall see visions, and your old men shall dream dreams; even on My bondslaves, both men and women, I will in those days pour forth of My Spirit and they shall prophesy. And I will grant wonders in the sky above and signs on the earth below, blood, and fire, and vapor of smoke. The sun will be turned into darkness and the moon into blood." (Acts 2:16–20 NASB)

The Bible says that when the listeners heard this they were pierced in their hearts. Why? It was because they had seen these prophecies fulfilled before their eyes. Previously on the day of Jesus's crucifixion, they saw the sun supernaturally darkened. Many believe there was a lunar eclipse (a blood moon) that night, as it was a full moon at Passover when Jesus was crucified. And now, they were certainly witnessing the infilling of the Holy Spirit in the believers. As a result, three thousand souls entered the kingdom that day.

It is likely that within our lifetimes we will see the fulfillment of prophecies. If we utilize them in the same manner as Peter did, vast multitudes will come to saving faith in Jesus. However, we must know the prophecies. We will discuss some of these in chapter six: Eyes Wide Open.

Indeed, God desires that we extend his offer of peace with him to the whole world. It is our honor to personally hand out the invitations. Let us take advantage of this honor God is giving us while we have the opportunity.

WHAT CAN I DO?

Every Christian can pray for missions, give to missions, support individual missionaries, or go to the mission field themselves. He wants to reward all who are involved in missionary work. Christ's primary commission to us as his Church (the Great Commission) is to make disciples of all people groups (Matthew 28:19). It is a responsibility he gave to each of us, not just to those currently on the mission field. Our default position as Christians is to go. In a sense, we are all called to a mission field. We need a special calling if we are to stay home. If we stay, however, we still are obligated and commanded to be a part of the Great Commission by means of prayer, giving, and local evangelism. We should all ask our Father how he wants us to participate.

Learning about missions is the first step in the process. Many churches have wonderful continuing education classes on missions available. Take one. Learning the history and theory of missions makes one more effective and strategic at prayer and giving.

In 1886, the Student Volunteer Missionary movement was started. It was enormously successful.[11] The concept of college-aged students leading the missionary charge still remains a powerful model. Like young members of the military, Christians of this age group have the enthusiasm and vigor for spiritual adventure. Groups like Youth With A Mission (YWAM), InterVarsity Christian Fellowship, Campus Crusade, and other similar organizations are the modern equivalents of the Student Volunteer movement. I recommend everyone reading this book to pray and ask where and how God wants you to become active, regardless of age. Student mission organizations, as well as all mission organizations, need volunteers to support, encourage, and fund those in the field.

EVENTUALLY, GOD FULFILLS THE GREAT COMMISSION

There is yet another point to be made about evangelism. It is easy to become almost depressed and have a guilt trip laid on us by the responsibility of the Great Commission given to the Church and the daunting task of taking the gospel around the world—hence, determining when Jesus comes back. Praise God that this is *not* the case, and we should not feel this way.

Is God ultimately limited by man's efforts and man's time frame? Indeed, God has given the Church the Great Commission to take the gospel around the world, and those who do will be rewarded. But does this mean that God must limit his end-of-the-age time frame for man to fully accomplish this? Can he not return at his second coming before the Great Commission is fully accomplished by man? The answer is YES he can, and the following is an explanation.

Related to evangelism, keep in mind that God is fair and just, and ultimately he will fulfill the Great Commission on earth in a way that allows him to control the timing of his return at his appointed time. His will is not constrained by man as to his timing of the end of the age and his coming again. Yes, he wants *us* to spread the gospel, and he will richly reward those who are so called, but God, ultimately, does not leave it to man to assume all the responsibility and control of the timing of accomplishing this. It is under his control and timing. An often overlooked verse in Revelation clarifies how God will accomplish this:

> And I saw another *angel flying in midheaven* [before God's wrath is unleashed on earth], having an *eternal gospel to preach to those who live on the earth*, and to every nation and tribe and tongue and people; and he said with a loud voice, "Fear God, and give Him glory, because the hour of His judgment has come; worship Him who made the heaven and the earth and sea and springs of waters." (Revelation 14:6–7 NASB, emphasis and clarification mine)

From the above passage in Revelation, we see that God will send, at the end of the age, an angel "flying in midheaven" around the world to present the "eternal gospel" to mankind. For this to be effective, all will hear it and understand it (a small task for God). In this sense, God fulfills the Great Commission. Hence, everyone will be "without excuse" to *not* have trusted in Jesus for their salvation.

In addition to evangelism outreach by the Church, God offers the possibility of salvation to everyone, even if not directly contacted by a missionary. Many people in the world are not so contacted. But God is fair and just and has provided natural revelation as a witness to himself as the Creator, from observing nature. David confirms this natural revelation in Psalm 19:

> The *heavens are telling of the story of God*; and their expanse is declaring the work of His hands. Day to day pours forth speech, and night to night reveals knowledge. There is no speech, nor are there words; their voice is not heard. *Their line has gone out through all the earth*, and their utterances to the end of the world. (Psalm 19:1–4 NASB, emphasis mine)

God knows the hearts of men and women who seek him. Each will be judged by the "light they have received" during their lives on earth. Salvation is only through Jesus, and sometimes God will reveal him to one who seeks him, by a dream or vision at night. Many missionary reports of this occurring in the Middle East are surfacing. Other times, God may cause a missionary to be sent specifically to an individual to share the gospel.

Critics say God is not fair. He is. At the final judgment of the wicked, all will admit their guilt and bow their knee and declare that Jesus is Lord. But salvation is only through Jesus, and one must put their trust in his salvation during this lifetime on earth. We have the privilege of sharing the gospel and, with the working of the Holy Spirit, leading someone to Jesus before they pass on from this life.

GO-FOR-BROKE ATTITUDE

Anyone involved in planning a wedding knows tensions rise the closer you get to the date. The week before the wedding is similar to the two-minute warning in a football game. Normal strategies that worked in the first fifty-eight minutes of the game are put aside. Bigger risks are taken, and the pace of play sometimes becomes frantic. In a wedding situation, this may involve a DJ backing out at the last minute or problems with the flowers, etc.

We should expect that as the date of our wedding with Christ approaches, a similar increase in the pace of the problems and opportunities will occur. I believe we are already seeing this happen in our world. Economically, the world is teetering on disaster. Politically, the rise of ISIS and Muslim extremism has gripped the world in a fist of terror. The resumption of tensions between the USA and Russia is now worse than at any time in the last fifty years. What should be our response to these pressures? Will we be willing to accept more risk? Should we be assuming a go-for-broke attitude when it comes to Christ's return since it seems evident that the world is increasingly breaking down anyway?

I am not a date setter—someone who tries to pinpoint the exact time of the return of Christ. I think that type of thinking is dangerous (see chapter five: Don't Believe the Movies). However, signs seem to indicate that we may well be the final generation before Jesus returns. Even if we are not, every generation needs to act as if they are.

What would a go-for-broke attitude look like in our lives? If we truly believed we had been given the two-minute warning, would we pray more, give more, and do more? Would we completely sell out for Christ, committing every fiber of our being to making him known? Certainly, it would involve increased attention to missions. We have also seen in chapter two that the American Church is asleep. So, it would also involve attempting to wake up the Church.

What would a go-for-broke attitude look like in our churches? In his landmark book, *Not a Fan* (Zondervan, 2011), Kyle Idleman discusses Jesus's approach to church growth: "It wasn't the size of the crowd Jesus cared about, it was their commitment." Would we fearlessly preach the complete gospel of the first and second comings of Christ without worrying about those it would offend? Would we dramatically up the ante on creating sold-out followers of Christ, rather than simply filling our pews with not-fully-committed *fans* of the Master? Would all of us be able to sign testimonies like the ones that litter Idleman's book that say, "My name is . . . , and I am not a fan," and then go on to describe really engaged commitment to following Jesus?

This little book, *Are We Ready For Jesus?*, has been written for just these purposes. It is meant to be given to friends and to pastors—your own and others. It is also meant to be preached by pastors, as well as given to denominational presidents, elders, and board members. Most church leaders do not yet realize that the Church is asleep, and they are the key to waking it up. Most churches are not yet in the two-minute warning mode. They need to get there quickly.

Our ministry, Ready for Jesus Ministries, is dedicated to helping folks like you spread the word. We realize that many laypersons feel ill-equipped to speak to our busy church leaders about taking time from their schedules to read a book like this. On our website (www.arewereadyforjesus.com) we have a downloadable and printable letter and several video links. These resources put into words and pictures what many of us may find difficult to express in a face-to-face meeting. We also have a page where you can inexpensively order additional copies of the book for distribution. The website also gives suggestions on how to approach church leaders to spread the message.

Christianity has morphed into a religion of defense, not offense; into a movement that relies on politics and fleshly approaches, not spiritual warfare. But time is short, and we need to get back to our first-century roots and go-for-broke commitment. What do we have to lose?

> For whoever desires to save his life will lose it, but whoever loses his life for My sake and the gospel's will save it. (Mark 8:35 NASB)

A Spotless Bride

As I waited for our wedding day to approach, it was easy to be faithful to my fiancée. She should have expected no less. If you love someone, you will be faithful. Jesus expects no less of us in our relationship to him. Peter discusses how watching for Jesus's return leads to righteousness.

> Since all these things are to be destroyed in this way [on the day of the Lord], what sort of people ought you to be *in holy conduct and godliness*, looking for and hastening the coming of the day of God . . . Therefore, beloved, since you look for these things, be diligent to be found by Him in peace, spotless and blameless. (2 Peter 3:11–12, 14 NASB, clarification and emphasis mine)

Love of the world is adultery to Christ. Love of money, illicit sex, entertainment, politics, human praise, and materialism are all love of the world. We need to trust in God and seek him only. This is part of the go-for-broke approach we need to take. We don't have time for distractions.

Love of America is part of our problem as well. While we are blessed to live here, and need to use our citizenship to protect America as best we are able, we are never to forget where our true citizenship lies—in God's kingdom.

> Brethren, join in following my example, and note those who so walk, as you have us for a pattern. For many walk, of whom I have told you often, and now tell you even weeping, that they are the enemies of the cross of Christ: whose end is destruction, whose god is their belly, and whose glory is in their shame—*who set their mind on earthly things. For our citizenship is in heaven, from which we also eagerly wait for the Savior*, the Lord Jesus Christ. (Philippians 3:17–20 NKJV, emphasis mine)

I notice with interest how our citizenship in the kingdom of heaven is linked in this verse to Jesus's return. I also notice that the enemies of Jesus are those who seek their own pleasure and glory. Those who set their minds on earthly solutions to problems are his enemies as well. We need to pray that we not fall into this trap. The Christian media perpetrates the vision that we should primarily seek earthly, political solutions to our spiritual problems. The wise virgins from chapter two have oil for their lamps (the Holy Spirit.) We need to seek his timing and his solutions as we prepare the way of the Lord.

The Marriage Ceremony

Finally, after all the waiting and preparation, Jesus will return for his bride, the Church. Revelation contains a passage that describes the wedding ceremony that takes place in heaven between the Church and the Lord. This occurs after the rapture of the Church.

> After these things I heard something like a loud voice of a great multitude in heaven, saying, "Hallelujah! Salvation and glory and power belong to our God . . . Let us rejoice and be

glad and give the glory to Him, for *the marriage of the Lamb* has come and His bride has made herself *ready*." It was given to her to clothe herself in fine linen, bright and clean; for the fine linen is the righteous acts of the saints. Then he said to me, "Write, 'Blessed are those who are invited to the *marriage supper of the Lamb.*'" (Revelation 19:1, 7–9 NASB, emphasis mine)

The next passage in Revelation describes Jesus and the great army of God returning to the earth to do battle with Satan and his forces of evil.

And I saw heaven opened, and behold, a white horse, and He who sat on it is called Faithful and True, and in righteousness He judges and wages war. (Revelation 19:11 NASB)

Here's an interesting thought. Jewish marriage laws require a groom to not go to war for one year after his marriage. Is it likely that Jesus and the bride of Christ will remain in heaven for one year after the rapture of the Church and prior to returning to the earth to fight Satan's forces? Because this one-year period is prescribed in scripture, I assume it is extremely likely.

When a man takes a new wife, he shall not go out with the army nor be charged with any duty; he shall be free at home *one year* and shall give happiness to his wife whom he has taken. (Deuteronomy 24:5 NASB, emphasis mine)

SUMMARY

All signs are that Jesus is coming soon. Our engagement period is almost over. In this brief, chaotic period before his return, we need to adjust our attitude from fear to joy and focus on what is truly important.

The basic steps for getting ready for Jesus from chapter four are:

1. We must assume an attitude of joy:
   Our bridegroom is returning. Despite persecution we should be joyful.

2. We must invite as many as possible to the wedding feast:
   We need to assume a missionary mindset. Focus should be on those in the 10/40 Window.

3. We should utilize *apocalyptic evangelism:*
   Prophecies are soon to be fulfilled. We need to point others to Christ by utilizing them.

4. Time is short:
   We must assume a go-for-broke approach to life.

5. We need to be faithful:
   We must live "sold-out" lives for Jesus.

In chapter five, we will discuss an important aspect of preparation for Jesus's return. We need to learn how to avoid deception.

CHAPTER FIVE

DON'T BELIEVE THE MOVIES:

HOW TO AVOID DECEPTION

See to it that no one misleads you.
(Matthew 24:4 NASB)

Human beings are incredibly visually oriented. Advertisers know this and use it to their advantage. The human eye is designed to detect change as a protective mechanism. If a saber-toothed tiger was rustling in the bush and our ancestor's eyes detected the movement, it might have saved his life. TV advertisers cash in on this need to watch for movement. Stand outside your home at night while a TV is on and watch the glow. Notice how it seems as if the TV is flashing. This is the number of changes per minute the programmers and advertisers have set for what you are watching. They know if they do not change the angle of the scene, they will lose your attention. TV programmers set numerous changes per minute so viewers are drawn to the program and cannot easily look away. This makes TV addictive. Biology created by God is utilized by TV programmers for their own purposes. Our visual nature is well known by God. That is why in Psalms it says: "I will set no worthless thing before my eyes" (Psalm 101:3 NASB).

For this reason, Christian books and movies have had an enormous effect on the Church, especially in the area of shaping our view of Jesus's return. The most pivotal book (and movie) of all time in this regard is probably *The Late Great Planet Earth* (1970) by Hal Lindsey and Carole Carlson.[12] The *New York Times* called the book: "No. 1 best seller of the decade." A number of my middle-aged friends came to faith in Christ after reading the book and watching the movie of the same name narrated by Orson Welles. In and of itself this is a wonderful testimony about the power of prophecy to evangelize.

However, if the theology behind any movie is faulty, great damage can be done. We should not be surprised when we encounter false teaching. When Jesus's disciples asked about his return, the first warning he gave us was about deception. "And Jesus answered and said to them, 'See to it that no one misleads you'" (Matthew 24:4 NASB).

It is interesting that the Christian media has misled us by giving us greatly mistaken views of when Jesus's return will occur. If we are going to be ready, we need a biblical view.

The Late Great Planet Earth and a later book by Lindsey and Carlson predicted the 1980s would be the final decade before Jesus's return.[13] In combination with *88 Reasons Why the Rapture Will Be in 1988* by Edgar Whisenant, these books galvanized a generation to prepare for Jesus's return. Unfortunately, they were both badly mistaken. The generation of churchgoers led astray by this erroneous date setting vowed, *We won't get burned again.* The effect of this deception is still being felt in the Church today. Many current church leaders were among the generation that was misled. The pendulum that had swung to the side of preparing for the rapture has swung back the other way. Many of these leaders want nothing to do with prophetic teaching in fear of being deceived.

That is the great danger of the Church gaining its understanding of Jesus's return from popular novels and movies. If the theology behind the media (books and movies) is faulty, the Church acquires a mistaken view of what is to come. Unfortunately, in today's consumer-driven churches, reading and studying the Bible is less common than perhaps at any time in Christian history. Media has become a huge source of the Church's understanding of Jesus's return. Could this be a cause of the Church becoming drowsy and falling asleep? I believe it is one of the causes. Look at the effect that date setting had in the popular Christian books of the 1970s and 1980s. Many of today's church leaders were just beginning their walk with

Jesus at that time. After being misled by the date setters, they have avoided teaching about Jesus's return to prevent possibly misleading others with false teaching. The effect on the Church has been enormous. If the leaders are not focused on Jesus's return, their churches won't be focused on it either.

It Is Not For You to Know

Let's take a closer look at date setting because it is likely that large numbers of new books and movies will be setting more dates in the near future. Unfortunately, this is nothing new. Date setting or trying to predict the return of Christ has a long and erroneous history. This limited list shows some of the highlights (or lowlights) of these mistaken attempts at prognostication.

Expected Date	Prognosticator	Notes
AD 50	Thessalonians	2 Thess. 2 indicates they believed the day of the Lord had already come and they had missed it.
AD 500	Hippolytus	
AD 1836	John Wesley	
AD 1844	William Miller/Millerites	Referred to as the "Great Disappointment." The Millerites eventually became the Seventh-day Adventists.
AD 1874	Jehovah Witnesses	After failing in 1874, the Witnesses later predicted 1914.
AD 1891	Joseph Smith/Mormons	
AD 1988	Edgar Whisenant	
AD 2000 or AD 2060	Sir Isaac Newton	
AD 2011	Harold Camping	After failing to correctly predict Christ's return in May 2011, Camping predicted October 2011.

Date Setting[14] [15]

Several predictions of Jesus's return are still in the future.

Expected Date	Prognosticator	Notes
AD 2015	Mark Blitz	Based on Blitz's *Blood Moon* interpretation
AD 2028	Kent Hovind	Written in prison
AD 2036	Tim Warner	Presented in the book, *The Time of the End*, an amazingly scholarly work utilizing the genealogies found in Genesis and other clues from Scripture to date all of the days of man from Adam to Jesus's return.

Future Date Setting[16]

My personal opinion is date setting is dangerous for the Church. That hasn't stopped Christian writers from doing it, however, because of the itchy ear syndrome. All Christians are interested in knowing the day and year of Jesus's return. Our ears itch when we hear a new theory about it. We shouldn't put anyone down for this interest. The disciples asked Jesus two questions about future prophetic events and both involved the question of timing.

> As He was sitting on the Mount of Olives, the disciples came to Him privately, saying, "Tell us, when will these things happen, and what will be the sign of your coming, and of the end of the age?" (Matthew 24:3 NASB)

> So when they had come together, they were asking Him, saying, "Lord, is it at this time you are restoring the kingdom to Israel?" (Acts 1:6 NASB)

However, Jesus's reply to the last question by the disciples should tell us all we need to know about date setting.

> He said to them, "*It is not for you to know* times or epochs which the Father has fixed by His own authority; but you will receive power when the Holy Spirit has come upon you; and you shall be My witnesses both in Jerusalem, and in all Judea and Samaria, and even to the remotest part of the earth." (Acts 1:7–8 NASB, emphasis mine)

Date setting has two potential negative results. If the date setter predicts a date that is sooner than the return of Jesus, he is labeled a false prophet, and rightly so. This negates much if not all of the person's teaching. It can also result in disillusionment on the part of his or her followers. We saw how this disillusionment affected the Church after the authors' prediction of the year of Jesus's return in *The Late Great Planet Earth* (1970), which obviously didn't happen.

The second negative result will occur if the date setter predicts a date that is after Christ's return. This result is worse than the first. Everyone following the prediction will be surprised by Jesus's return, and the result will be the same as if they were asleep—they won't be prepared. The only date setting result that is favorable is if we predict it exactly, which Jesus seems to indicate isn't possible as to the exact day and year.

CAN WE "SEE" HIS RETURN COMING?

In my opinion we shouldn't seek to set an exact date for Christ's return and should shun popular books or movies that try to accomplish this. They are dangerous. Even though we can't know the exact date of Christ's return, does this mean we can't know the season of his return? I not only believe we can see the return of Christ approaching by watching for the signs he gave us, I believe he has commanded us to watch for these signs! "Watch therefore! For you do not know what hour your Lord is coming," says Matthew 24:42 NKJV. Jesus not only commands us to watch, he says the reason we need to watch is we don't know the hour he is coming. This makes perfect sense. Since we don't have an exact date, we need to be watchful for the signs Jesus gave us so we have an idea of when he is coming and can prepare.

I find it interesting that the Greek word translated "know" in most translations of verse 42 above is *iodate*, which means "know because you have seen." In the NKJV a slightly different Greek word is found in the original text, *eido*, which means simply "to see." Utilizing these translations, a possibly better interpretation of Matthew 24:42 is: "So watch because you haven't seen what hour your Lord is coming yet."

This makes sense. We will devote the entire next chapter of this book to the subject of being watchful. Remember, being watchful is the opposite of being asleep! You may be thinking, *What if we aren't the last generation and his coming is delayed? Are we watching for nothing?* Every generation needs to prepare as if it is the last generation, for we do not know what hour and day our Lord is coming.

WE DO NOT KNOW WHAT HOUR OUR LORD IS COMING!

THE OTHER MOVIE; THE OTHER PROBLEM

The Late Great Planet Earth has probably had the greatest effect on the Church of all popular books and movies about prophecy. A close second is the *Left Behind* series. For those living in a vacuum for the last twenty years, *Left Behind* is a series of sixteen, quick-paced action books by Tim LaHaye and Jerry Jenkins detailing the lives of those left behind by the rapture of the Church. In addition to the book series, there are three movies and a video game. In 2014, a major Hollywood production of the series was released starring Nicolas Cage.[17]

As with *The Late Great Planet Earth*, many Christians today came to faith after reading this book series. I anticipate the 2014 movie will have an equally dramatic effect on the eternal destiny of many. Hallelujah! The positive effects of biblically based prophecy movies on society can be tremendous. I am praying God's Spirit moves mightily.

Unfortunately, just as we explained with *The Late Great Planet Earth*, there is a downside to popular movies and books about prophecy. If the theology behind them is faulty, the Church can be misled. This is especially true in our modern media era where believers gain most of their knowledge from YouTube, movies, and social media, and not directly from the Bible. Believers cannot test the spirits regarding theories about Jesus's return if they aren't regularly reading God's Word.

> Beloved, do not believe every spirit, but test the spirits to see whether they are from God, because many false prophets have gone out into the world. (1 John 4:1 NASB)

We already saw how an unbiblical approach to date setting in *The Late Great Planet Earth* was one cause of the drowsiness of the Church. Could there be an unbiblical theology in the *Left Behind* series by Tim LaHaye and Jerry Jenkins that is also causing the Church to sleep?

I believe this theory in *Left Behind* is the primary reason the Church is asleep!

Is your mind racing yet? What theory in *Left Behind* is unbiblical and could cause the Church to sleep? Perhaps you read the books yourself and found little or nothing wrong with them. To see what this theory is, let's consider the effects of sleep on the Church that we looked at in chapter two. Perhaps we will find a clue there.

- Few churches would openly discuss or preach the return of Jesus on a regular basis. Some would claim opposing theories on Jesus's return are too controversial and would avoid them.

Some would view discussing or preaching the return of Jesus as irrelevant because they believe we won't see any difficult times.

- Churches would choose to spend the majority of their monies on local efforts rather than on missions.

- Churchgoers would live earthly lives concentrating on entertainment, materialism, and pleasure rather than seeking God's kingdom first.

Jesus's return would be thought of as some vague, distant event by nearly all churchgoers with no real relevance to everyday life.

In my opinion, there is only one theory about Jesus's return that could cause each and every one of these effects. There is only one theory that could cause churchgoers and church leaders to consider Jesus's return a nonissue and not worth discussing on a regular basis. There is only one theory in the modern Church that could cause Jesus's return to be anything but the most important, anticipated, longed-for, and prayed-for event ever.

That theory is that we won't see any difficult times before he returns. If Christians believe they won't personally be affected by the hard times preceding Jesus's return, they are tempted to tune out and may think, *Why worry about what won't affect me personally? My Jesus would never do that to me.* This faulty theory is the *pretribulation rapture* further described in the following sections of this chapter.

"My Jesus Would Never Do That to Me"

The Christians in the Middle East, who are currently being beheaded and crucified by the Islamic State because of their refusal to deny Christ, would not want to hear us in the West say, *My Jesus would never do that to me.* Praise God for the faith of these persecuted believers! Only the rich and privileged Western Church believes we won't see hard times. The persecuted Church in China, Indonesia, the Middle East, and Africa already are experiencing pain, suffering, and death because they worship Jesus.

These Christians are not asleep. They are praying and working daily to bring back our king, their deliverer! Why would *their Jesus* allow them to be persecuted and not those of us in the West? Why would *their Jesus* exclude us? In fact, why would *my Jesus* remove his workers, his Church, from the earth at the very moment they are needed most? As we learned in the previous chapter, we are entering the two-minute warning and need every Christian engaged.

In the trailer for the newest *Left Behind* movie, a young girl whose mother was raptured says, *The God my mother talked about would never do something like this.* These are almost the same words as *My Jesus would never do that to me.* Obviously, she is wrong in the fictional movie. But, let's imagine what would have happened if the rapture hadn't come when expected. What if her mother and all the others snatched away in the movie's fictional rapture had to endure persecution as well? What if all were left behind and had to face the Antichrist? How would they respond? In chapter two we learned this verse from the illustration of the head of the house and the thief.

> For this reason you also must be ready; for the Son of Man is coming at an hour when you do not think He will. (Matthew 24:44 NASB)

The American Protestant Church teaches this means Jesus can come for us at any time and that there are no prophecies left unfulfilled before Jesus returns to rapture believers. They believe his return is imminent. But what if this verse actually means he is not coming when the Church expects him? What if it means he is coming *after* the Antichrist is revealed? This would explain why Jesus links being ready with his unexpected return. If he is coming after the "great falling away" and the Antichrist, we would have to prepare for these things. Amazingly, scripture teaches clearly this is exactly what will happen.

Now we request you, brethren, *with regard to the coming of our Lord Jesus Christ and our gathering together to Him*, that you not be quickly shaken from your composure or be disturbed either by a spirit or a message or a letter as if from us, to the effect that the day of the Lord has come. Let no one in any way deceive you, for *it will not come unless the apostasy comes first, and the man of lawlessness is revealed*, the son of destruction, who opposes and exalts himself above every so-called god or object of worship, so that he takes his seat in the temple of God, displaying himself as being God. (2 Thessalonians 2:1–4 NASB, emphasis mine)

BOTH THE GREAT APOSTASY AND THE REVEALING

OF THE ANTICHRIST WILL COME

BEFORE THE RAPTURE.

SAY IT ISN'T SO!

Perhaps your mind is spinning and you are thinking of throwing this book into the trash. You may be saying, *Nelson, I don't even want to think about these things. My Jesus would never do that to me. But you already showed me how that isn't true. But my seminary professor, my pastor, my denomination, and everyone I know teaches we will be snatched away before the hard times start. Wait, you already showed me they are all asleep! Nelson, please say it isn't so! This is too scary.*

Before you stop reading, let me say two things. First, it isn't nearly as scary as you think, and I'll prove that to you at the end of this chapter. Second, Jesus commands us to think about these things whether it's comfortable to think about them or not.

> For though we walk in the flesh, we do not war according to the flesh, for the weapons of our warfare are not of the flesh, but divinely powerful for the destruction of fortresses. We are destroying speculations and every lofty thing raised up against the knowledge of God, and *we are taking every thought captive to the obedience of Christ,* and we are ready to punish all disobedience, whenever your obedience is complete. You are looking at things as they are outwardly. If anyone is confident in himself that he is Christ's, let him consider this again within himself. (2 Corinthians 10:3–7 NASB, emphasis mine)

You may know these verses, even have them memorized, and don't think they apply to the rapture. Yes, they do. They apply to all our theories about the Christian faith. We are to take *every* thought captive and make it obey Christ. This includes both sinful thoughts and theological thoughts. If our thoughts about Jesus's return are flawed, they can be among the most destructive thoughts possible.

Notice two things about this scripture's instruction. First, Paul equates thoughts with spiritual warfare. If a thought doesn't come from God, it comes from our flesh or Satan. Second, notice he tells us we are looking at things outwardly (in the flesh), not inwardly (by the spirit). The emotion of fear you may have felt reading this chapter is a fleshly thing. Remember we discussed how it is Satan who causes us to fear the return of Jesus, not God. Join me in a short prayer:

> Lord Jesus, in the words of the father whose child you healed, we do believe, but *help our unbelief.* Lord, this is so difficult for us. Comfort us and help us to know what really is true. Help us put aside our flesh and the fear that Satan wishes to use to paralyze us. Let your perfect love cast out all fear. Amen.

AN ACADEMIC EXERCISE

I believe there is nothing more potentially divisive in the Church than the timing of the rapture. Because of this, nearly every popular Christian book written refers to discussing the timing of the rapture as an academic argument and avoids it. Yet here we are discussing it. This book is a bit different; I warned you. We are discussing this issue because it is critically important. It is much, much more important than a disagreement about who has interpreted scripture correctly.

If those who believe we will be raptured before hard times are wrong, what would be the result? Have you considered it? Will the Church enter its greatest challenge totally unprepared? If the opposite is true, what would be the result? If we prepare to face the Antichrist but are raptured first, will any harm come to the Church?

For this reason, if you are going to believe and teach that we will be raptured before the hard times start, you better be correct. Millions of souls hang in the balance, and God will certainly judge us if we lead them astray!

America's first family of Christianity, Rev. and Mrs. Billy Graham, took a similar approach when discussing preparation for hard times. The late Ruth Graham had this to say in a letter to Dave MacPherson, "I would rather prepare myself to go through the tribulation and be happily surprised by an unexpected rapture than expect to be raptured only to find myself going through the tribulation."[18] Billy had this to say on page 72 of Sam Shoemaker's book *Under New Management*, "Perhaps the Holy Spirit is getting His Church ready for a trial and tribulation such as the world has never known."

Most American pastors and seminaries teach what is known as a pretribulation rapture. This position teaches that the rapture will occur before any hard times begin and before the tribulation starts. They teach it as fact as if it is unquestionably scripturally based. Who wants to discuss or debate this? Eighty percent of your church might not show up the following Sunday, and the pastor may be fired by the elders or the denomination. Arguing against the pretribulation rapture is heresy to some and is confrontational to all because of fear.

But is this discussion academic, or could there be a spiritual battle taking place? Let's return to the concept that false theological theories could very well be satanic.

> But the Spirit *explicitly* says that in later times some will fall away from the faith, paying attention to deceitful spirits and doctrines. (1 Timothy 4:1 NASB, emphasis mine)

Notice the Spirit is unequivocal: in these last days some will fall away from the faith because of faulty doctrines. This is an incredibly strong statement. Could the pretribulation rapture theory be one of these? It is one of the most cherished theories of the American Church. But what if it is wrong? What if there is even a miniscule chance of it being wrong? What might occur?

- **The American Church would not be prepared to face hard times.**

  They are expecting to be raptured before these times hit. How would Christians respond if they have been taught their whole lives they will not face these predicted hard times and they do? What if the rapture doesn't come when they expect? (Jesus already told us it won't come when we expect it.) I believe most would feel so misled by the teaching of their churches they would seriously question their faith in Jesus himself.

- **The American Church would not be prepared to face the Antichrist.**

  What would happen in America if the Antichrist comes to power before the rapture? What if everyone is given the choice of taking the mark of the Beast or not being able to buy or sell? (See Revelation 13:16–17.) That would mean no food, clothing, or shelter. In a moment of weakness would they take the mark? Would they be more likely to take it if they had been taught their whole life they wouldn't face this choice?

- **The American Church would not be prepared to give up their lives.**

  What if the choice is beheading or denying Christ as it currently is in Iraq at the hands of the Islamic State? What would Americans do? Are we ready to face such a choice? Would we deny Christ?

Corrie ten Boom was a Christian survivor of Nazi concentration camps and a lifelong missionary. She was not a fan of the pretribulation rapture theory and had the following to say about preparing for persecution:

> In China, the Christians were told, *don't worry, before the tribulation comes you will be translated—raptured.* Then came a terrible persecution. Millions of Christians were tortured to death. Later I heard a Bishop from China say, sadly, *we have failed. We should have made the people strong for persecution rather than telling them Jesus would come first. Tell the people how to be strong in times of persecution, how to stand when the tribulation comes—to stand and not faint.* I feel I have a divine mandate to go and tell the people of this world that it is possible to be strong in the Lord Jesus Christ. We are in training for the tribulation, but more than sixty percent of the Body of Christ across the world has already entered into the tribulation. There is no way to escape it. We are next. Since I have already gone through prison for Jesus's sake, and since I met the Bishop in China, now every time I read a good Bible text I think, *hey, I can use that in the time of tribulation.* Then I write it down and learn it by heart.[19]

Can you see now why this theory is not an academic question? Let's return to the illustration of the head of the house and the thief we looked at in chapter two.

> But be sure of this, that if the head of the house had known at what time of the night the thief was coming, he would have been on the alert and would not have allowed his house to be broken into. *For this reason you also must be ready;* for the Son of Man is coming at an hour when you do not think He will. (Matthew 24:43–44 NASB, emphasis mine)

The thief is coming to kill, steal, and destroy. What is preventing our churches from being alert for the thief? Is it a theory that we won't face the thief? Does the theory that we won't see hard times help the thief accomplish his evil purposes? These are tough questions that anyone teaching the pretribulation rapture position must answer.

This is why we must argue for or against the theory that we won't face the Antichrist and the "great apostasy." Everything is at stake. It is not an academic question. It is not an argument of who is right and who is wrong. It is the reason why we are asleep, and it's a question of eternal life and death.

The Bible Study No One Wants To Do

In 2004, I was diagnosed with prostate cancer. I was one of the youngest patients my physician had ever seen with that disease. Fortunately, he was not asleep because of my age, and I was diagnosed early. I was treated and the cancer is gone. Praise God! Finding out that there is no pretribulation rapture is like finding out you have cancer. You don't want to know. But I can tell you this, now that I am cancer-free, I am so glad I was correctly diagnosed!

Examining whether or not there is a pretribulation rapture is the Bible study no one wants to do. Most believers in the pretribulation rapture don't really want to know they may be wrong. But ask yourself if you would rather find out now or when it is too late to prepare. I can tell you this, it is much better to be prepared just as it is much better to be diagnosed (as I was with cancer).

So let us begin our study with a brief history of the pretribulation rapture. Many probably don't realize it, but the pretribulation rapture theory is relatively new. The majority of the early church fathers taught the rapture would occur at the end of the tribulation and that the Church would experience tribulation. Less than two hundred years ago, John Nelson Darby (I like his middle name) articulated the first widely circulated view that the rapture would occur before the tribulation. The pretribulation rapture gained widespread enthusiasm with the publication of the Scofield Reference Bible in 1909 which mentioned it in its notes. In 1957, John Walvoord of the Dallas Theological Seminary published *The Rapture Question*, giving biblical support to the idea of a rapture occurring prior to the last day. Finally in the 1970s, this concept became mainstream with the publication and promotion of the flawed theology of *The Late Great Planet Earth*. Today, the pretribulation rapture is the predominant view within the American Protestant Church.[20]

I am sure most are shocked to learn this view of Jesus's return has been widely popular for only fifty years. I was. When I became a Christian, it was the only theory about the timing of Jesus's return that I was taught. It wasn't until later, through personal Bible study, that I learned there were other views of the timing of the rapture.

Here is a second fact that I'm sure you will find unbelievable. There isn't one verse in the Bible that says the rapture will occur prior to the tribulation and prior to hard times beginning. The position of the pretribulation rapture is based entirely on inference. Certain facts in the Bible are assembled, and from those facts, believers in this theory assume the rapture happens prior to the hard times beginning.

You have seen the pretribulation rapture theory is potentially dangerous if not true. Now that you know it has only been universally popular for less than fifty years and is based solely in inference, I am sure you are beginning to see why this book is exploring the question of the validity of that theory.

Where We Agree

The theory of a pretribulation rapture originated because of questions regarding the traditional view of the rapture—which is that Jesus would return on the last physical day of the tribulation. The most important of these questions involved God's wrath. The Bible teaches that at some point during the tribulation, God will pour out his punishment on the ungodly. This is known as God's wrath. Two well-known Bible passages show clearly that Christians won't experience the wrath of God.

> Wait for His Son from heaven, whom He raised from the dead, that is Jesus, who rescues us from the wrath to come. (1 Thessalonians 1:10 NASB)

> For God has not destined us for wrath, but for obtaining salvation through our Lord Jesus Christ. (1 Thessalonians 5:9 NASB)

This is straightforward instruction for the Church. We will not experience God's wrath. Nearly all Christians believe the pouring out of God's wrath is synonymous with the phrase the "day of the Lord" in scripture. Traditionally, this was thought to be a single day at the end of the tribulation on which Jesus descends to earth and crushes the powers of evil. Pretribulation rapture theory holds that the day of the Lord is more complex and longer than a single day. This book agrees.

Finally, pretribulation rapture theory teaches that the *parousia* (Greek for "coming," "arrival," or "presence") of Christ is a complex event with two stages. The first is the rapture of believers, and the second is the physical return of Christ to the earth to punish the wicked still living at that time on earth and to usher in his kingdom. This book also teaches a complex *parousia*, or presence of Christ, featuring the rapture and a later physical return of Christ.

Considering this book agrees with the mainstream teaching on the rapture in so many areas, it is surprising there are any differences at all.

The differences may seem slight, but they are profound. Those differences change everything in regard to the timing of the return of our king.

WHERE WE DISAGREE

The main point of disagreement between this book and the mainstream Protestant Church is in regard to when the day of the Lord begins. If you remember, we have just learned that the day of the Lord is the period of time when God's wrath is poured out on the ungodly. We also learned that the rapture will occur prior to the day of the Lord, so its timing is crucial. Pretribulation rapture theory teaches the day of the Lord (God's wrath) begins with the start of the tribulation and that the entire seven-year tribulation is God's wrath.

This book teaches that the day of the Lord begins later, after the seventh seal of the book of Revelation (Revelation 8:1–5), and that the wrath which believers experience prior to this point is the wrath of Satan and the Antichrist against the elect of God. This sounds like an extremely academic difference, but as we have shown, the implications of this argument are anything but academic. How we answer this argument and how we teach the Church has the potential to affect the eternal destiny of millions of churchgoers. It is the responsibility of every Christian to understand this argument, and teach those under their leadership appropriately. This is an incredibly big responsibility. God will judge us all on how we respond.

WHAT IS THE MAINSTREAM VIEW OF THE CHURCH ON THE TRIBULATION?

The mainstream view of the Church is that the entire last seven-year period, commonly known as the tribulation, is the day of the Lord. We need to first have a firm understanding of this period if we are to determine if the rapture occurs before or during this period.

This last seven-year period is foretold in scripture as the Seventieth Week of Daniel's prophecy of the seventy *shabua*. *Shabua* is a Hebrew word and means a period of seven years. During the first six years, normal agricultural work could take place. During the seventh *shmita* year, God had specified that the land should be given a sabbatical rest (Lev. 23:1–7). This was to mirror the seven days of creation, and the normal week of six days of work followed by a Sabbath day of rest Lev. 23:3. Daniel's prophecy specified that seventy cycles of these *shabua* were allotted for Jerusalem and the Jews.

> Seventy weeks have been decreed for your people and your holy city, to finish the transgression, to make an end of sin, to make atonement for iniquity, to bring in everlasting righteousness, to seal up vision and prophecy and to anoint the most holy place. So you are to know and discern that from the issuing of a decree to restore and rebuild Jerusalem until *Messiah the Prince* there will be seven weeks and sixty-two weeks; it will be built again, with plaza and moat, even in times of distress. *Then after the sixty-two weeks the Messiah will be cut off* and have nothing. (Daniel 9:24–26 NASB, emphasis mine)

The first sixty-nine of these *shabua* were fulfilled the day Jesus rode into Jerusalem on a donkey revealing himself as Messiah. The prophecy also foretold the Messiah would die but not for himself. (He died for us all!) Finally, the prophecy declares there will be one future *shabua* (seven-year period), which is commonly called the tribulation (the Seventieth Week of Daniel). In addition, a description of the lineage of the Antichrist is given—he will come from the people-group of the actual soldiers who destroyed the temple (70 AD), as well as some details of his activities during the last seven-year period.

> The people of the prince who is to come will destroy the city and the sanctuary. And its end will come with a flood; even to the end there will be war; desolations are determined. And he will make a firm covenant with the many for one week, but in the middle of the week he will put a stop to sacrifice and grain

offering; and on the wing of abominations will come one who makes desolate, even until a complete destruction, one that is decreed, is poured out on the one who makes desolate. (Daniel 9:26–27 NASB)

In review, there will be a seven year period prior to the return of Jesus. This period commonly goes by the name of the Tribulation or the 70ᵗʰ Week of Daniel. At the midpoint of this period, the figure known as the Antichrist will eliminate the Jewish sacrificial system and set up an "abomination" in the Temple of God. We know from other texts that we will study in Chapter Six that the last half of this seven year period is known as the Great Tribulation. This is a period of persecution and martyrdom. Finally at the end of the period, Jesus will return to punish evil and set up his Kingdom on Earth.

Now that we have a working understanding of the seven-year tribulation period, let's examine the rapture. There are many proofs that the rapture occurs during the seven-year tribulation, not before it. We will look at five of them.

THE CELESTIAL/EARTHLY DISTURBANCE EVENT

Pretribulation rapture theory states that the entire seven-year tribulation period is the day of the Lord (God's wrath). This book teaches that the day of the Lord begins later. Is there a scripture that can clearly show us who is correct? Yes, there is.

> I will display wonders in the sky and on the earth, blood, fire and columns of smoke. The sun will be turned into darkness and the moon into blood *before the great and awesome Day of the LORD comes.* (Joel 2:30–31 NASB, emphasis mine)

God has said an event will occur that theologians call the "celestial/earthly disturbance." This passage from Joel shows it will occur before the day of the Lord (God's wrath). This makes it a time marker for the wrath of God. This event is not a ho-hum, everyday occurrence. God says he will display wonders in the sky and on the earth. This same Hebrew word is used in the Old Testament for the signs and judgments God brought against Egypt and Pharaoh. This event will be unmistakably a God thing. It will not be a collection of eclipses or similar natural phenomenon. It will be wondrous and terrifying.

The celestial/earthly disturbance is detailed in other scriptural passages. If we assemble all five passages which describe these celestial and earthly events, we should be able to determine when the wrath of God actually does occur rather than simply assume it begins at the start of the tribulation. The following four verses also provide further details of this event.

> Wail, for the day of the Lord is near! It will come as destruction from the Almighty. Therefore all hands will fall limp, and every man's heart will melt. They will be terrified, pains and anguish will take hold of them; they will writhe like a woman in labor, they will look at one another in astonishment, their faces aflame. Behold, the day of the Lord is coming, cruel, with fury and burning anger, to make the land a desolation; and He will exterminate its sinners from it. For the stars of heaven and their constellations will not flash forth their light; the sun will be dark when it rises and the moon will not shed its light. Thus I will punish the world for its evil and the wicked for their iniquity; I will also put an end to the arrogance of the proud and abase the haughtiness of the ruthless. I will make mortal man scarcer than pure gold and mankind than the gold of Ophir. Therefore I will make the heavens tremble, and the earth will be shaken from its place at the fury of the Lord of hosts. (Isaiah 13:6–13 NASB)

> But immediately after the tribulation of those days the sun will be darkened, and the moon will not give its light, and the stars will fall from the sky, and the powers of the heavens will

be shaken. And then the sign of the Son of Man will appear in the sky, and then all the tribes of the earth will mourn, and they will see the Son of Man coming on the clouds of the sky with power and great glory. And He will send forth His angels with a great trumpet and they will gather together His elect from the four winds, from one end of the sky to the other. (Matthew 24:29–31 NASB)

There will be signs in sun and moon and stars, and on the earth dismay among nations, in perplexity at the roaring of the sea and the waves, men fainting from fear and the expectation of the things which are coming upon the world; for the powers of the heavens will be shaken. Then they will see the Son of Man coming in a cloud with power and great glory. But when these things begin to take place, straighten up and lift up your heads, because your redemption is drawing near. (Luke 21:25–28 NASB)

I looked when He broke the sixth seal, and there was a great earthquake; and the sun became black as sackcloth made of hair, and the whole moon became like blood; and the stars of the sky fell to the earth, as a fig tree casts its unripe figs when shaken by a great wind. The sky was split apart like a scroll when it is rolled up, and every mountain and island were moved out of their places. Then the kings of the earth and the great men and the commanders and the rich and the strong and every slave and free man hid themselves in the caves and among the rocks of the mountains; and they said to the mountains and to the rocks, "Fall on us and hide us from the presence of Him who sits on the throne, and from the wrath of the Lamb; for the great day of their wrath has come, and who is able to stand?" (Revelation 6:12–17 NASB)

Three of these four passages demonstrate that Jesus's visible return (*Parousia*) will begin *after* this celestial/earthly disturbance event. (The Revelation passage uses the word *presence*, which is also the Greek word *Parousia*.) From a detailed study of all these verses, we should be able to time mark the beginning of God's wrath and the rapture which occurs with Jesus's *parousia*. The following table lists the details of each of the five passages.

Column1	Joel 2:30–31	Isa. 13:6–13	Matthew 24:29	Luke 21:25–26	Rev. 6:12–14
Sun	Darkness	Dark when it rises	Darkened	Signs in the sun	Black as sackcloth
Moon	Color of blood	Not shed its light	Not give its light	Signs in the moon	Color of blood
Stars		Not flash forth light	Fall from the sky	Signs in the stars	Fall from the sky
Heavens		Heavens tremble	Powers of the heavens will be shaken. Sign of the Son of Man will appear.	Powers of the heavens will be shaken.	Sky split and rolled up like a scroll
Seas				Roaring of the waves (tsunami?)	
Earth	Blood, fire, and columns of smoke (volcanoes?)	Earth shaken			Earthquake; every mountain and island moved
Righteous				Lift your head; your redemption is near.	
Wicked		Hands go limp; hearts melt		Perplexity among the nations; men fainting	Hid in caves and asked rocks to fall on them
What Proceeds	Pouring out of God's Spirit		The great tribulation	Jerusalem trampled at the midpoint of the tribulation	Fifth seal broken at midpoint of tribulation
What Follows	Day of the Lord, the wrath of God	Day of the Lord, the wrath of God	Son of Man comes on the clouds with great glory and his angels gather the elect.	Son of Man comes on the clouds with great glory.	Wrath of the one who sits on the throne and the Lamb has come.

Celestial Earthly Disturbance Event

What is immediately obvious from studying this table is all five passages picture the same event. It will be awesome and terrifying. In addition to the sun and moon being darkened, meteors will fall, and there will be an earthquake, volcanoes, and tsunamis. The hearts of the wicked will melt at the sight, and they will hide themselves in caves.

Anyone who claims the blood moon tetrad experienced on earth in 2014 and 2015 fulfills these scriptures is not reading all the related passages. This will be a one-of-a-kind event.

In our study in this chapter we are most interested in what proceeds and what follows this event. It is obvious from Joel, Isaiah, and Revelation that the day of the Lord (God's wrath) follows this event. It is a time marker for the beginning of the day of the Lord. Very interestingly, it is also apparent that after this event and prior to God's wrath being poured out, Jesus returns on the clouds and his angels gather the elect (seen in heaven in Revelation 7:9–17). This is the rapture!

What precedes the celestial/earthly disturbance is also fascinating. The great tribulation, as mentioned by Jesus (Matthew 24:21) comes first. We also see this detailed in the passages in Matthew, Luke, and Revelation. Placing all five visions of this same event side-by-side gives us this amazingly comprehensive look at the events surrounding Jesus's return and reveals details not seen in one passage.

THE RAPTURE OCCURS AFTER THE TRIBULATION AND PRIOR TO THE WRATH OF GOD.

To say other than that the rapture occurs after the tribulation and prior to the wrath of God, a Christian would have to deny that these passages are speaking of the same event. No serious student of scripture can deny the facts presented on the table, which clearly show the amazing consistent fingerprint of this singular event. Only someone fighting to remain asleep could deny that the rapture occurs following the sixth seal of Revelation (Revelation 6:12–17), immediately after the celestial/earthly disturbance.

Are Paul's Vision and Jesus's Vision the Same?

When asked for scripture verses that give evidence for a pretribulation rapture, adherents of this theory always point to Paul's words in 1 Thessalonians 4. This certainly is a picture of the rapture, but it gives no sense of timing in and of itself and, hence, no real support for a pretribulation rapture.

> For this we say to you by the word of the Lord, that we who are alive and remain until the coming of the Lord, will not precede those who have fallen asleep. For the Lord Himself will descend from heaven with a shout, with the voice of the archangel and with the trumpet of God, and the dead in Christ will rise first. Then we who are alive and remain will be caught up together with them in the clouds to meet the Lord in the air, and so we shall always be with the Lord. Therefore comfort one another with these words. (1 Thessalonians 4:15–18 NASB)

Jesus provides us a vision of the rapture as well in Matthew 24, his teaching on the Mount of Olives.

> But immediately after the tribulation of those days the sun will be darkened, and the moon will not give its light, and the stars will fall from the sky, and the powers of the heavens will be shaken. And then the sign of the Son of Man will appear in the sky, and then all the tribes of the earth will mourn, and they will see the Son of Man coming on the clouds of the sky with power and great glory. And He will send forth His angels with a great trumpet and they will gather together His elect from the four winds, from one end of the sky to the other. (Matthew 24:29–31 NASB)

Those who promote a pretribulation rapture claim Jesus's vision in Matthew 24 is an event other than the rapture. They claim it is the second coming when Jesus physically sets foot on the Mount of Olives. This is an incredibly important discussion because Jesus's prophecy in Matthew 24 clearly states the event he describes occurs after the tribulation. ("But immediately **after** the tribulation . . .") If it is shown to be the same event as in Paul's vision (in 1 Thessalonians 4:15–18), then the pretribulation rapture is disproven.

Let's look at the similarities.

- First, at the very outset of Paul's vision, he uses the phrase, "We say this by way of the word of the Lord." In the Old Testament this would have meant that God spoke to Paul directly. In the New Testament, this phrase means what Paul was teaching were the direct words of Jesus. Where would Paul have gotten this direct teaching? From the Olivet Discourse, of course! Paul got his teaching from the very passage to which we are comparing it.

- Paul uses a phrase, "we who are alive and remain," twice in this passage. The Greek words imply the people survived a great tragedy during which many others died. This is certainly a match with the great tribulation.

- Notice that both visions include angels.

- Both visions include a trumpet blast.

- Notice in both visions Christ is in the air.

- Notice both visions use the term "together" in reference to the saints. In Paul's vision he says those who remain and the resurrected will be "caught up together." In Jesus's vision the angels gather *together* the elect.

- In Mark's version of the Olivet Discourse, a slightly different wording gives us more insight. "He will send forth the angels, and will gather together His elect from the four winds, *from the farthest end of the earth to the farthest end of heaven*" (Mark 13:27 NASB, emphasis mine). This shows movement from

90

earth to heaven. It demonstrates the rapture, just as in Paul's version where the elect are "caught up."

- In Jesus's vision, he mentions "the sign of the Son of Man." The disciples had prompted the entire Olivet Discourse by asking what would be the sign of his coming. The sign of Jesus's return, or *Parousia*, is the brightness of his coming that will flash from the east to west. The sign marks the beginning of the *Parousia*, not the end.

These multiple similarities show that the rapture visions of Paul and Jesus are one and the same and occur *after* the start of the tribulation, during the Seventieth Week of Daniel, and not pretribulation.

VULTURES AND THE RAPTURE

Interestingly, the Greek word translated "gather together" above is also used earlier in Matthew 24:28. It is found in a strange illustration that the Church does not fully understand. Matthew 24:28 (NASB) says, "Wherever the corpse is, there the vultures will gather." Whenever we don't understand a passage, it is likely that a mistaken theology is blocking our understanding. I believe that is the case with this verse. The Church does not understand because this verse refers to the resurrection that will occur *after* the great tribulation. Their view that the resurrection and rapture occur prior to the tribulation prevents them from seeing what this verse truly means.

In context, this verse is a summation of a lengthy passage Jesus gives on the Great Tribulation. This passage begins in verse 15 and ends with verse 28. Immediately prior in verse 27, we find the "sign of the son of man" referenced, the Shekinah glory of Jesus coming on the clouds, which is the Jesus' *Parousia,* or presence.

The word translated "vultures" is actually a Greek word that means "eagles." In Revelation this same word is used to symbolize angels in Revelation 4:7, 8:13, and 12:14. The word translated "gather" is the same

Greek word that we have seen before and means "gather together." In Jesus's vision of the rapture, he used this word to describe how the angels gather together the elect from the four winds. This short illustration in Matthew 24:28 pictures the same event. It is critically important to note the angels are gathering the dead who died knowing Christ (the corpse), which occurs at the resurrection. This occurs immediately *before* the rapture of the living (1 Thessalonians 4:16) and is further overwhelming proof that the rapture occurs after the start of the great tribulation, during which the Antichrist will be killing both Jews and Christians (Revelation 6:9–11).

WHAT ABOUT REVELATION 3:10?

Many of those who trust a Pre-Tribulation timing of the rapture point to this verse (Rev. 3:10) as one of the best proofs of that position. It appears to say that God will keep certain Christians (in the Philadelphia Church) from having to face the Tribulation, but is that what it really says?

> Because you have kept the word of my perseverance, I also will
> *keep* you from the hour of *testing*, that hour which is about to
> come upon the whole world, to test those who dwell on the
> earth. (Rev. 3:10 NASB, emphasis mine)

The words on this page are an English translation of the original verse that was written in Greek. Two of those Greek words hold the key to understanding. "Keep" is the Greek word *téreó* meaning "to guard" or to "keep watch over." It does not mean to remove from. God does not promise to remove the Philadelphia church from testing. The verse says that members of this church will be guarded from the trial or will be guarded in the midst of the trial. It does not say they will be removed from the trial.

The Greek word translated "testing" is *peirasmos* meaning trial, test, or temptation. It does not say tribulation. This is the same word Jesus used in the Lord's Prayer when he said, "Lead us not into temptation."

The clear meaning of this verse in my opinion is that God will guard the believers during their temptation during the "great falling away" which occurs after the midpoint of the Tribulation period. This verse does not prove a Pre-Tribulation rapture despite the fact I have heard hundreds of teachers claim that it does.

It Will Not Come Unless

To be complete, we also must include Paul's other description of the rapture in his second epistle to the Thessalonians that includes references to timing. This text is probably the most undisputable proof that the rapture is not pretribulational.

> Now we request you, brethren, *with regard to the coming of our Lord Jesus Christ and our gathering together to Him,* that you not be quickly shaken from your composure or be disturbed either by a spirit or a message or a letter as if from us, to the effect that the day of the Lord has come. Let no one in any way deceive you, for *it will not come unless* the apostasy comes first, and the man of lawlessness is revealed, the son of destruction who opposes and exalts himself above every so-called god or object of worship, so that he takes his seat in the temple of God, displaying himself as being God. (2 Thessalonians 2:1–4 NASB, emphasis mine)

This passage clearly shows that the abomination that causes desolation (the revealing of the man of lawlessness) at the midpoint of the tribulation occurs prior to the rapture and the start of the day of the Lord. This passage proves that the pretribulation rapture theory is wrong when it claims the entire tribulation is the day of the Lord. This passage also clearly shows that Christians will face the "great apostasy" and the Antichrist because Jesus's coming and our gathering together to him (the rapture) will not come until *after* those things happen.

Also, it should be noted that the phrase "gathering together" in 2 Thessalonians is exactly the same Greek word as was used in the passages we looked at earlier in Matthew 24: 28 and 31. This is even further proof that both this passage and the passages in Matthew 24 refer to the rapture, and that the rapture occurs after the start of the great tribulation which begins at the midpoint of the Seventieth Week of Daniel.

THE PRETRIBULATONAL RESPONSE

If this passage of scripture is so overwhelming clear, why are there any proponents of the pretribulation rapture? There is a debate within the Church about the meaning and translation of one verse in the passage above, "Let no one in any way deceive you, for it will not come unless the *apostasy* comes first, and the man of lawlessness is revealed" (2 Thess. 2:3 NASB, emphasis mine). Those who favor a pretribulation timing for the rapture claim the Greek word translated apostasy is a code-word for the rapture. Those favoring a timing of the rapture after the great tribulation claim the word means rebellion or an abandoning of the faith.

Those favoring pretribulation rapture timing also claim that there is a sequential order to the events listed in this verse. They claim that the event translated as "apostasy" comes first and the revealing of the Antichrist comes second. This makes complete sense for them because in order for the rapture to be pretribulational, it must precede the revealing of the Antichrist at the midpoint of the Tribulation period. To support that position they point to the verse and the fact that Paul, who wrote the verse, used the word "first" immediately after the word translated "apostasy."

This thinking may seem logical but if we do a strict, contextual examination of Paul's writing, he consistently uses "first then" if he means a sequence of events. He always uses both words in combination. It is a consistent pattern in is writings. An example is found in the most famous rapture verse of all, "The dead in Christ will rise *first. Then* we who are alive, who are left, will be suddenly caught up together" (1 Thess. 4: 16-

17 NASB, emphasis mine). Because Paul does not use the word "then" in conjunction with the word "first," we can be assured that the apostasy and the revealing of the Antichrist are two events that happen at the same time and both precede the rapture. This contextual proof by itself disproves the pretribulational rapture placing the rapture after the midpoint of the tribulation period not at the beginning.

IS THE PROPER TRANSLATION RAPTURE OR APOSTASY?

The Greek word translated "apostasy" in this passage is "apostasia." Because the entire pretribulation rapture theory hangs on this one definition, let's look at *Strong's Dictionary's* definition of the word:

> apostasia: defection, revolt
>
> Original Word: ἀποστασία, ας, ἡ
> Part of Speech: Noun, Feminine
> Short Definition: defection, apostasy
> Definition: defection, apostasy, revolt.[21]

HELP'S Word-studies provides additional information on this word:

> **646** *apostasía* (from 868 */aphístēmi*, "leave, depart," which is derived from 575 */apó*, "away from" and 2476 */histémi*, "stand") – properly, departure (implying *desertion*); *apostasy* – literally, "a leaving, from a previous *standing*."[22]

Since this definition is abundantly clear, why is there a debate as to the meaning of the word? Several ancient 15th century English translations of the Bible claimed the word "apostasia" meant "the departure." These mis-translations were based on one of the words apostasia was derived from: "aphistemi" which does mean departure. This mis-translation led those who support a Pre-Tribulation rapture to say that this word is a code-word for rapture: "the departure." This view is mistaken. The word "apostasia" is undoubtedly translated as rebellion from the faith.

This word is also used in the Book of Acts and this second use cements this proper translation.

> You see, brother, how many thousands there are among the Jews of those who have believed, and they are all zealous for the Law; and they have been told about you, that you are teaching all the Jews who are among the Gentiles to *forsake (apostasia)* Moses, telling them not to circumcise their children nor to walk according to the customs. (Acts 21: 20-21 NASB, clarification and emphasis mine)

In this passage, the elders of the Church at Jerusalem were speaking to Paul. They told him that the faithful Jews in Jerusalem had been told that he was teaching the gentiles to rebel against the faith ("apostasia") of Moses. This exact match of meaning proves that apostasia means rebellion from the faith or falling away from the faith.

There is even further contextual proof that the definition proved is accurate. Paul supports this meaning of apostasia in the following passage:

> The one whose coming is in accord with the activity of Satan, with all power and signs and false wonders, and with all the *deception* of wickedness (The Antichrist) for those who perish, because they did not receive the love of the truth so as to be saved. For this reason God will send upon them *a deluding influence* so that they will believe what is false, in order that they all may be judged who did not believe the truth, but took pleasure in wickedness. (2 Thess. 2: 9-12 NASB, clarification and emphasis mine)

Is Paul talking about those who were already opposed to Christ or is this passage about those falling away in the great apostasy? Those already opposed to Christ don't need a deluding influence to oppose Christ, they are already fallen. In this passage Paul is discussing the reason that former professing saints will fall away in the great apostasy. This is critical because Paul would not have included this follow-up passage explaining the great apostasy unless he had just mentioned it a few verses earlier. Otherwise Paul would have simply been entering a random thought into his letter. This contextual proof further supports our position that a pretribulational rapture is absolutely without merit.

WHY IS THIS SO IMPORTANT?

I am sorry that the last proof against a pretribulational rapture was so complex. I went into detail about this proof and the preceding ones because knowing the truth about a pretribulational rapture is of extreme importance. Why is it important? It is overwhelmingly important because if Christians and churches realize this *one fact*, they will prepare to face the Antichrist and his persecutions. To not prepare is spiritual suicide.

WHAT WILL THE RAPTURE LOOK LIKE?

If the rapture isn't pretribulational, what is it? This book teaches the rapture will occur after the sixth seal of Revelation and before the seventh seal of Revelation. This is known as the pre-wrath rapture. There are three excellent reference books that explain this theory in detail:

- *Antichrist Before the Day of the Lord* by Alan Kurschner (Eschatos Publishing, 2013);

- *Examining the Pre-Wrath Rapture of the Church* by Marvin Rosenthal and Kevin Howard (Thomas Nelson, 1994);

- *The Last Shofar!* by Joseph Lenard and Donald Zoller (Xulon Press, 2014).

I highly recommend all these books.

This following schematic is what the prewrath rapture looks like.

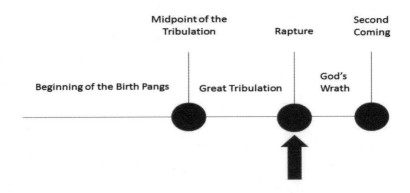

The Prewrath Rapture

Let's return to a description of the tribulation period first. It is universally understood by nearly all Christians that the tribulation will be seven years long and divided into two halves, each 1260 days (forty-two prophetic Jewish months of thirty days each) long. At the midpoint the Antichrist will be revealed at an event known as the abomination of desolation. Jesus refers us to this event, and so does Paul. The last half of the tribulation has a special name given to it by Jesus: the Great Tribulation.

> Therefore when you see the ABOMINATION OF DESOLATION which was spoken of through Daniel the prophet, standing in the holy place (let the reader understand) . . . (Matthew 24:15 NASB)

> The man of lawlessness is revealed, the son of destruction, who opposes and exalts himself above every so-called god or object of worship, so that he takes his seat in the temple of God, displaying himself as being God. (2 Thessalonians 2:3–4 NASB)

In this event the Antichrist will enter the reconstructed temple of God in Jerusalem and exalt himself over every other god, including the one true God. Immediately after this event, the great tribulation will occur. This is the point where the great apostasy begins as well, 1260 days into the tribulation (Daniel 9:27). Believers will be asked to bow down and worship the Antichrist. Those who do not will be persecuted and killed. This period is the wrath of Satan and the Antichrist against God's people and will be cut short for believers in Jesus by the rapture.

We have seen earlier in this chapter that the rapture occurs after these central events but before God pours out *his* wrath on the Antichrist and his empire. God's wrath is the wrath that scripture has promised that we believers will not have to endure. Presently, many believers all over the world are already experiencing Satan's wrath.

We are unsure when the rapture takes place during this great tribulation period. What we do know is that Jesus comes for his Church sooner than the full final 1260 days.

> For then there will be a great tribulation, such as has not occurred since the beginning of the world until now, nor ever will. Unless those days had been cut short, no life would have been saved; but for the sake of the elect *those days* [the 1260] *will be cut short.* (Matthew 24:21–22 NASB, emphasis mine)

The Last Shofar!—*What the Fall Feasts of the Lord Are Telling the Church* by Joseph Lenard and Donald Zoller (Xulon Press, 2014) integrates the fall Feasts of the Lord (Lev. 23) into the chronology of the second coming of Jesus—that the rapture will occur on a Feast of Trumpets and Jesus's physical return on Yom Kippur, about a year after the rapture. If, indeed, Jesus will return at the appointed time of the Feast of Trumpets for the rapture, this is further evidence that the doctrine of the imminent return of Jesus (the pretribulation rapture position that Jesus can come at any time) is not true and further undermines the pretribulation position.

DO NOT BE SURPRISED

Peter tells us to not be surprised if we are persecuted.

> Beloved, *do not be surprised* at the fiery ordeal among you, which comes upon you for your testing, as though some strange thing were happening to you; but to the degree that you share the sufferings of Christ, *keep on rejoicing*, so that also at the revelation of His glory you may rejoice with exultation. If you are reviled for the name of Christ, you are blessed, because the Spirit of glory and of God rests on you. (1 Peter 4:12–14 NASB, emphasis mine)

There is that concept again: we are to rejoice if we are persecuted. The Greek word translated "with exultation" means to jump up and down with joy. Few Christians react to potential persecution by jumping up and down. However, the Bible says we are to view any potential persecution with Jesus's return in mind. Peter continues this most instructive teaching.

> If anyone suffers as a Christian, he is not to be ashamed, but is to glorify God in this name. For it is time for judgment to begin with the household of God; and if it begins with us first, what will be the outcome for those who do not obey the gospel of God? "And if it is with difficulty that the righteous is saved, what will become of the godless man and the sinner?" Therefore, *those also who suffer according to the will of God shall entrust their souls to a faithful Creator in doing what is right.* (1 Peter 4:16–19 NASB)

It is God's plan that judgment is to begin with the household of God. We are to trust God in this persecution because he understands all and sees all. He will do what is right for us. I realize this is hard to understand with fleshly eyes and minds. But God is telling us to not be surprised when this happens, but to trust him. The end of the story is worth it.

Escape

For those who trust him, God will make a way of escape.

> But keep on the alert at all times, praying that you may have
> strength to escape all these things that are about to take place
> and to stand before the Son of Man. (Luke 21:36 NASB)

The Greek words translated "may have strength" mean "will be found worthy." Some Christians will be worthy to escape the persecution. Jesus tells us the same thing in Revelation.

> Because you have kept the word of my perseverance, I also will
> keep you from the hour of testing, that hour which is about
> to come upon the whole world, to test those who dwell on the
> earth. (Revelation 3:10 NASB)

What do these verses say are the reasons God will keep his children from the fiery trial of his wrath? First we are to be watchful; we are to keep on the alert. (We will study that concept in chapter six.) Second, we are to pray specifically that we are found worthy. And third, we are to patiently endure the little things now to escape the trial that is coming.

In the verse immediately preceding the word translated "keep" is a Greek word that means to "keep guard." This does not speak of removing us from the trial but rather guarding us through it. It may be that the escape we are granted is that we are given grace to endure the trial. The following verse also mentions escape, but it also speaks of endurance rather than removal.

> No temptation has overtaken you but such as is common to
> man; and God is faithful, who will not allow you to be tempt-
> ed beyond what you are able, but with the temptation will
> provide the way of escape also, so that you will be able to
> endure it. (1 Corinthians 10:13 NASB)

God will be faithful. If we see all these things, we will know without any doubt that Christ is returning in less than 1260 days. That is incredible. For me it is a thought that will help me endure any trial. At that time, it will not only be the two-minute warning, but it will be the last ten seconds of the game. As a former football player, I would gladly endure a 250-pound linebacker tackling me if it meant scoring the winning touchdown. That is what the persecutions of those days will be like.

Corrie ten Boom, a Nazi concentration camp survivor, has this to say about gaining the strength to endure persecution, and I think it is wonderful insight:

> When I was a little girl I went to my father and said, *Daddy, I am afraid that I will never be strong enough to be a martyr for Jesus Christ.* "Tell me," said Father, "When you take a train trip to Amsterdam, when do I give you the money for the ticket? Three weeks before?" *No, Daddy, you give me the money for the ticket just before we get on the train.* "That is right," my father said, "and so it is with God's strength. Our Father in Heaven knows when you will need the strength to be a martyr for Jesus Christ. He will supply all you need — just in time."[23]

If we live to see those days, we will be part of God's great plan to redeem and restore the world. Participating in his great overthrow of evil will be an amazing opportunity. Certainly, it makes us anxious, but the end result is what we need to keep in mind. The king is coming, and our hope and eternal destiny are secure in him. Praise God.

> *Keep on rejoicing, so that also at the revelation of His glory you may rejoice with exultation* [you will jump up and down with joy!] (1 Peter 4:13 NASB, emphasis and clarification mine)

Summary

In this chapter we learned that incorrect Church doctrine can be a major source of deception. We learned that it is dangerous to attempt to set a specific date for the return of Christ and that we should attempt to avoid books and teachings that try to tickle our ears with proposed dates for that glorious day.

We also learned that potentially the most dangerous of all Church doctrines is the widely held pretribulation rapture theory. The danger of this theory is that if it is incorrect (and we have presented much evidence for this!), it will cause millions of Christians to not prepare for the tribulation and to be caught completely unaware.

The basic steps for getting ready for Jesus from this chapter are:

1. **We must avoid the deception of "date setting":**
    We should watch for signs of Jesus's return, but we must be careful not to assume we can know the day or hour of his return.

2. **We must avoid the deception of the *pretribulation rapture* theory:**
    The primary reason the Church is asleep is this mistaken theory.

3. **The *pretribulation rapture* theory is incredibly dangerous:**
    Christians deceived by this theory will be unprepared to face persecution, the great apostasy, and the Antichrist. Because they are unprepared, they may fall away from the faith.

In the next chapter we discuss Jesus's command to watch for prophesied events prior to his return. We also detail all the signs and events for which Jesus asks us to watch. It is important to know these signs and events so we are not caught unaware.

Chapter Six

Eyes Wide Open:

What to Watch For

And what I say to you, I say to all: Watch! (Mark 13:37 NKJV)

This summer our family adopted a brand new puppy. Toby was only three pounds when he came home and is as cute as can be. When he goes for a walk in our neighborhood, he attracts attention. Children run out of their houses just to pet him. One little girl asked, "Can he come inside to play?" Her dad gave a look that said, *I don't think he's potty trained yet!* Toby has inspired several families to adopt their own puppies.

Unfortunately, he attracted some negative attention as well. Six times this month we have encountered a coyote on our walks. The first time I saw one it had rained all day. The rain finally let up around nine p.m., and my dog and I went for our walk even though it was pitch black. We were about two hundred yards from our home when I heard an unearthly yelp. Turning around, I saw a coyote not more than twenty feet behind me. I yelled at it and waved my hands, but it just stared at me. I pulled my dog close by my side and started walking home. The coyote followed us, keeping his twenty-foot distance. I continued to yell at him, but to no avail. Fortunately, we made it home safe and sound.

I now carry a walking stick with me for our protection. I have lived in this neighborhood for eight years and up until this month was never observant on my walks. Now in the dark I am hyperobservant. I listen for every sound and look behind every bush.

That is how my Christian walk has been as well. Until ten years ago I never gave Jesus's return much serious thought. It was *pie in the sky in the great by and by* to me and nearly every other Christian I knew. I did not listen for every spiritual sound nor look behind every spiritual bush on my Christian walk. To be honest, I hoped Jesus wouldn't return too soon. I love my life, my family, and the work God has called me to and didn't want it to end just yet. I wouldn't be surprised if many reading this book feel the same way.

WHAT DOES "WATCH" MEAN?

Jesus commands us, however, that if we are going to be ready for his return we need to be watchful.

> Watch therefore, for you do not know when the master of the house is coming—in the evening, at midnight, at the crowing of the rooster, or in the morning—lest, coming suddenly, he find you sleeping. And what I say to you, I say to all: Watch! (Mark 13:35–37 NKJV)

What does the command "watch" mean, and what are its implications? *Webster's Dictionary* defines "watch" as "to look at (someone or something) for an amount of time and pay attention to what is happening." Common sense would dictate that this is also the meaning of the word found in the Bible.

Because of this definition, some who hold to the pretribulation rapture theory believe the passage in Mark applies only to saints who come to faith in Jesus after the rapture. Jesus contradicts this thinking by the simple phrase, "What I say to you [the disciples], I say to all." This includes all Christians, not just ones who come to faith after the rapture.

Some who hold to the pretribulation rapture theory say the Olivet Discourse applies only to the Jews. We discounted this position in chapter two. Clearly, Jesus's warning to watch is for everyone. All means *all.* Jesus was warning us that we are all to watch.

Because the position that the Olivet Discourse applies only to the Jews stands on such shaky ground, others choose to spiritualize the word *watch* to mean "to be careful to avoid temptation." They choose this meaning because if they chose Webster's definition, *watch* would imply being on the lookout for the signs of Jesus's return. Most ascribing to a pretribulation rapture theory don't believe we need to watch for signs because they believe his return is imminent. Dr. Thomas Ice (one of the world's leading proponents of a pretribulation rapture) states, "Imminence carries the sense that it could happen at any moment. Other things may happen before the imminent event, but nothing else must take place before it happens." Dr. Ice believes that no prophecies need to be fulfilled prior to Christ's return.[24]

Fortunately, we don't have to guess or even debate to know the biblical meaning. The Greek word translated "watch" in Mark 13 is *grēgoreó*, which means "to be vigilant and alert, as a guard on a night watch." This word does not mean being careful to remain pure, as many in the church teach. It means we must keep both eyes open and be observant.

"Watch" is most often found in passages related to Jesus's return. It was also used by Jesus when scolding the disciples after falling asleep on the night he was betrayed, "Could you not watch with Me one hour?" (Matthew 26:40 NKJV). Watching is the opposite of sleeping, as we learned in chapter two, and we find passages contrasting watching and sleeping throughout the Bible. In addition to the above passage from Mark, here are a few more examples:

> But concerning the times and the seasons, brethren, you have no need that I should write to you. For you yourselves know perfectly that the Day of the Lord so comes as a thief in the night. For when they say, "Peace and safety!" then sudden destruction comes upon them, as labor pains upon a pregnant woman. And they shall not escape. But you, brethren, are not in darkness, so that this Day should overtake you as a thief. You are all sons of light and sons of the day. We are not of the

night nor of darkness. Therefore let us not sleep, as others do, but let us watch and be sober. (1 Thessalonians 5:1–6 NKJV)

If you will not watch, I will come upon you as a thief, and you will not know what hour I will come upon you. (Revelation 3:3 NKJV)

Both of these references are interesting. They state that Jesus's return will not take us by surprise if we watch. It will not come upon us as a thief in the night if we're observant of the signs of his coming. This clear teaching is contrary to the view held by the majority of Christians: that the return of Jesus is imminent. We will see prophetic events occur, and, if we watch for them, we will know the season of Jesus's return. His very command to watch proves that prophetic events will occur before the rapture and that it isn't imminent. Indeed, there are events that must first occur, or why would we be commanded to watch? What would we be watching for?

A ROAD MAP TO JESUS'S RETURN

When Jesus's disciples asked him what would be the sign of his coming and the end of the age, Jesus responded with thirty-eight verses of prophecy and five parables. This complete sermon was his answer to their question! There isn't just one sign; the entire Olivet Discourse is the sign.

> # THE OLIVET DISCOURSE IS A
> # CHRONOLOGIC ROAD MAP OF EVENTS.

Interestingly, within this sermon are over thirty separate references to seeing, watching, hearing, and being observant. A listing of these events will give a basic idea of the type of things for which Jesus wants us to watch.

- Matthew 24:4; Mark 13:5 (NASB): "See to it that no one misleads you." The Greek is *blépō*, "be observant."

- Matthew 24:6; Mark 13:7 (NASB): "You will be hearing of wars and rumors of wars."

- Mark 13:9 (NASB): "But be on your guard; for they will deliver you to the courts." The Greek is again *blépō*, "be observant."

- Matthew 24:15; Mark 13:14 (NASB): "Therefore when you see the Abomination of Desolation . . ."

- Luke 21:20 (NASB): "But when you see Jerusalem surrounded by armies, then recognize that her desolation is near."

- Matthew 24:23; Mark 13:21 (NASB): "Then if anyone says to you, 'Behold, here is the Christ,' or 'There He is,' do not believe him."

- Matthew 24:27 (NASB): "For just as the lightning comes from the east and flashes even to the west, so will the coming of the Son of Man be." The Greek word for "flashes" is *phainō*, "appears."

- Luke 21:11, 25 (NASB): "And there will be terrors and great signs from heaven . . . There will be signs in sun and moon and stars."

- Matthew 24:30; Mark 13:26; Luke 21:27 (NASB): "And then the sign of the Son of Man will appear in the sky, and then all the tribes of the earth will mourn, and they will see the Son of Man coming on the clouds of the sky with power and great glory."

- Luke 21:28 (NASB): "But when these things begin to take place, straighten up and lift up your heads, because your redemption is drawing near."

- Matthew 24:33; Mark 13:29; Luke 21:31 (NASB): "When you see all these things, recognize that He is near, right at the door."

- Matthew 24:36; Mark 13:32 (NASB): "But of that day and hour no one knows." The Greek for "knows" is *oidate*, "know because you have seen."

- Matthew 24:42 (NASB): "Therefore be on the alert, for you do not know which day your Lord is coming." The Greek for "know" is *oidate*, "know because you have seen."

- Matthew 24:43 (NASB): "But be sure of this, that if the head of the house had known at what time of the night the thief was coming, he would have been on the alert." The Greek for "known" here is *eido*, "had seen."

- Mark 13:33 (NKJV): "Take heed, watch and pray; for you do not know when the time is." The Greek word for "heed" is *blépō*, "be observant."

- Mark 13:34–37 (NASB): "It is like a man, away on a journey, who upon leaving his house and putting his slaves in charge, assigning to each one his task, also commanded the doorkeeper to stay on the alert. Therefore be on the alert—for you do not know when the master of the house is coming, whether in the evening, at midnight, or when the rooster crows, or in the morning— in case he should come suddenly and find you asleep. What I say to you I say to all, 'Be on the alert.'" The Greek for "know" here is *oidate*, "know because you have seen."

- Luke 21:36 (NASB): "But keep on the alert at all times, praying that you may have strength to escape all these things that are about to take place."

- Matthew 25:6 (NASB): "Behold, the bridegroom!"

- Matthew 25:13 (NASB): "Be on the alert then, for you do not know the day nor the hour."

- Matthew 25:37–39, 44 (NASB): "Then the righteous will answer Him, 'Lord, when did we see You hungry, and feed You, or thirsty, and give You something to drink? And when did we see You a stranger, and invite You in, or naked, and clothe You? When did we see You sick, or in prison, and come to You? . . . Lord, when did we see You hungry, or thirsty, or a stranger, or naked, or sick, or in prison, and did not take care of You?'"

More than thirty separate references to being watchful are found in this one sermon! I was stunned myself when I counted them all. Jesus obviously wants us to keep watch. If you remember, being watchful is the opposite of being asleep! It is Jesus's primary command for us regarding preparing for his return.

We can group the references of things to watch for into several main categories. From these categories we can better understand for what we are to be alert as shown in the following chart.

Events	Description	Verses
The Fig Tree	Reformation of the nation of Israel	Matt. 24:32–35 Mark 13:28–32 Luke 21:29–33
Beginning of the Birth Pangs	Deception, war, rebellions, famine, disease, terrors, "seismos," heavenly signs	Matt. 24:4–8 Mark 13:5–8 Luke 21:8–11
Midpoint of the Tribulation	Abomination that causes desolation; armies surround Jerusalem	Matt. 24:15–21 Mark 13:14–20 Luke 21:20–24
Persecutions	We will be hated by all nations, and they will put some of us to death.	Matt. 24:9–14 Mark 13:9–13 Luke 21:12–19
Great Apostasy	Christians will betray each other	Matt. 24:10, 12, 43–51; Mark 13:12; Luke 21:16
False Messiahs and Lying Wonders	Some will say Jesus is in the desert or the inner room.	Matt. 24:4, 23–28 Mark 13:5, 21–22 Luke 21:8
Celestial/Earthly Disturbance	The sun and moon will darken, and stars will fall from the sky.	Matt. 24:29; Mark 13:24–25; Luke 21:11, 25–28
Rapture	Jesus will come on the clouds with great glory, and his angels will gather the elect.	Matt. 24:30–31 Mark 13:26-27
Judgment	Jesus gathers and judges the nations.	Matt. 25:31–46

The Signs of Jesus's Return

We can further group these events into those before the great tribulation, those during this period, and those after the great tribulation.

Timing	Events
Prior to the Great Tribulation	The fig tree
	The beginning of the birth pangs
During the Great Tribulation	Events at the midpoint
	Persecutions
	The great apostasy
	False messiahs and lying wonders
After the Great Tribulation	Cosmic signs
	The rapture
	The judgment

The Timing of the Signs of Christ's Return

Now that we've organized the signs, let's look at them individually to better understand them. Remember, watching is a primary way we prepare for Jesus's return.

THE FIG TREE

In the Olivet Discourse, Jesus went into meticulous detail to list the chronological events that will occur before his return. Then nearly at the end of his teaching, he dropped an enormous clue about what sign would signal the beginning of the events that would lead to his return.

> Now learn the parable from the fig tree: when its branch has already become tender and puts forth its leaves, you know that summer is near; so, you too, when you see all these things, recognize that He is near, right at the door. Truly I say to you, this generation will not pass away until all these things take place. Heaven and earth will pass away, but My words will not pass away. (Matthew 24:32–35 NASB)

To the modern Church, the surface meaning of this parable is Jesus's coming is near when the signs in the Olivet Discourse begin to be fulfilled. This is certainly one meaning of this parable. But there is a deeper symbolic meaning that gives us a clue to the "season" of his coming.

In order to find the deeper meaning of this parable, we must know what is being symbolized by the "fig tree" and "puts forth its leaves." The disciples understood that the fig tree represents the nation of Israel from references throughout the Old Testament. Here is an example from Hosea:

> Like grapes in the wilderness, I found Israel. Like the first fruit on the fig tree, in its first season. (Hosea 9:10 NRSV)

Jesus used this symbol several times in his teaching ministry. In Luke 13:6 he told a parable of a fig tree that bore no fruit and was chopped down. In Luke 6:44, when he told how one can know a tree based on its fruit, one of the trees was a fig tree. And in Mark 11:20–21, Jesus miraculously withered a fig tree that bore no figs. In all these instances, he used the fig tree as a symbol of Israel.

"Puts forth its leaves" pictures a tree sprouting leaves in the spring after lying dormant in winter. This is a perfect picture of Israel becoming a nation again in 1948 after lying dormant since AD 70, when it was defeated by Rome and its people scattered. Israel put forth its leaves when it once again became a nation. So, the first sign Jesus gives us, the time marker to let us know the season of his return, is the rebirth of the nation of Israel.

ISRAEL'S REBIRTH IS THE FIRST SIGN.

This sign has obviously already taken place. He is coming soon!

Some have used this sign to try and date set the return of Christ. The book, *88 Reasons the Rapture Will Be in 1988*, used these exact verses to set that erroneous date. Matthew 24:34 NASB says, "This generation will not pass away until all these things take place." This obviously does not refer to the generation alive at the time Jesus uttered them. Most believe it means the generation that saw Israel become a nation again, and this interpretation is most likely correct. We know that happened in 1948. The writer of *88 Reasons* felt this was the meaning and used some biblical reasoning to claim a generation is forty years. Adding forty years to 1948, he came to his errant conclusion of 1988. Others have claimed a generation to be seventy or eighty years, and surmise that Jesus will return in 2018 or 2028. Actually, it could mean whatever term of years that some of those alive in 1948 are still living. As of 2015 it has already been sixty-seven years since 1948. The point to be made is that it may not be too many more years until this sign related to the last generation is fulfilled and "all these things" described by Jesus in the Olivet Discourse take place.

I stand by my previous statement: date setting is dangerous. All of us, however, should agree that the first sign of Jesus's return has been fulfilled—Israel is a nation again.

THE BEGINNING OF THE BIRTH PANGS

Jesus then gave us a grouping of signs he referred to as the "beginning of the birth pangs." These are the next series of events on the chronologic road map given to us by Jesus.

> When he was sitting on the Mount of Olives, the disciples came to him privately, saying, "Tell us, when will this be, and what will be the sign of your coming and of the end of the age?" Jesus answered them, "Beware that no one leads you astray. For many will come in my name, saying, 'I am the Messiah!' and they will lead many astray. And you will hear of wars and rumors of wars; see that you are not alarmed; for this must take place, but the end is not yet. For nation will rise against nation, and kingdom against kingdom, and there will be famines and earthquakes in various places: all this is but the beginning of the birth pangs." (Matthew 24:3–8 NRSV)

In these six verses, Jesus summarizes a number of major events that will occur prior to his return. He calls this period "the beginning of the birth pangs." God's Word gives us wonderful analogies fashioned out of real life. Here Jesus relates the coming of his kingdom to the end of a pregnancy. The first stage is the birth pangs that occur prior to the great tribulation. Next are intense labor pains that equate to the great tribulation itself. Finally, the baby is born that equates to the return of Jesus, the resurrection, and the rapture. By calling this initial period the birth pangs, Jesus was recalling Isaiah's words:

> O LORD, in distress they sought you, they poured out a prayer when your chastening was on them. Like a woman with child, who writhes and cries out in her pangs when she is near her time . . . Your dead shall live, their corpses shall rise . . . and the earth will give birth to those long dead. (Isaiah 26:16–17, 19 NRSV)

Once the baby arrives, the mother forgets the pain of the process. The baby pictured here is the resurrection.

In Matthew, Jesus indicates this beginning of birth pangs period will be marked by the deception by false messiahs, a falling away of many Christians from the faith, wars and rumors of wars, famines, and earthquakes. In Luke 21:8–11, Jesus adds a few more items: rebellions, plagues, terrors, and signs in the heavens.

Many people equate these signs with the first three and a half years of the tribulation. Jesus does not tell us when these events begin. Because we have been freed from the pretribulation rapture mindset that says everything bad happens after the Church has been raptured, it is possible these traumatic events might begin prior to the seven-year tribulation. Some of these events may be about to occur at this very moment.

Do you now see how a mindset that believes the Church will not experience any hard times causes it to be asleep regarding the signs Jesus has given us? Very few Christians are watching or expecting the signs in this portion of scripture to occur at this time. It is this mindset that prevents the Church from obeying Jesus's command to watch.

WHERE SHOULD WE WATCH?

God has created a big world. Before we begin to watch for the birth pangs, we need to know where to look. Americans and Europeans have their eyes naturally drawn to their own countries. The Bible, however, was written in the Middle East and is Israel and Jerusalem-centric. It only makes sense that the majority of things Jesus commands us to watch for will take place in that area, not in the West.

Since the sign of the fig tree (the rebirth of the nation of Israel), constant struggle has taken place in the Middle East. We must ask if this is coincidence or part of God's plan for the return of Jesus. God promised the controversy over the ownership of Jerusalem would become the focus of world geopolitics:

> Behold, I will make Jerusalem a cup of drunkenness to all the
> surrounding peoples. (Zechariah 12:2 NKJV)

It makes sense that we should watch this area of the world closely. It also
makes sense that the Man of Sin, the Antichrist, will come out of this
general region. Again, God's Word confirms this is true. Micah and Isaiah
show he will be an Assyrian (from Syria, eastern Turkey, or northern Iraq).

> This One [Jesus] will be our peace. When the Assyrian invades
> our land, when he tramples on our citadels, then we will raise
> against him . . . and He will deliver us from the Assyrian when
> he attacks our land and when he tramples our territory. (Mi-
> cah 5:5–6 NASB, clarification mine)

> And the Assyrian will fall by a sword not of man, and a sword
> not of man will devour him. So he will not escape the sword.
> (Isaiah 31:8 NASB)

Additionally, John tells us the Antichrist will deny both the Father and the
Son, as Muslims do.

> Who is the liar but the one who denies that Jesus is the Christ?
> This is the antichrist, the one who denies the Father and the
> Son. (1 John 2:22 NASB)

All of these verses encourage us to watch the Middle East. Joel Richardson's recent book, *Mideast Beast—the Scriptural Case for an Islamic Antichrist* (WND Books, 2012), and Mark Davidson's recent book, *Daniel Revisited—Discovering the Four Mideast Signs Leading to the Antichrist* (West
Bow Press, 2013), are extremely helpful in making the case to "watch the
Middle East." Most of the following insights in this chapter are from these
two resources, and they are highly recommended.

IRAN, TURKEY, AND THE RISE OF THE ANTICHRIST

This subtitle alone may be shocking to you. Iran and Turkey are in the news every day. Might they have something to do with the rise of the Antichrist? Might those events be beginning right now? I believe they do, and they are, because the prophet Daniel tells us so.

The prophet Daniel describes the rise of the Antichrist in detail in Daniel 7 and 8. These passages deserve a great deal of attention and study. Traditionally, because these visions seemed similar to historic events, Christian scholars mistakenly thought they were prophecies of those historic events. This "close but not quite" (or "near" of a "near/far") fulfillment of a prophecy is known as a foreshadow. What the traditional views have missed were these two incredible verses:

> He [the angel Gabriel] said to me, "Son of man, understand that the *vision pertains to the time of the end* ." (Daniel 8:17 NASB, emphasis and clarification mine)

> He said, "Behold, I am going to let you know what will occur at the final period of the indignation, for it *pertains to the appointed time of the end.*" (Daniel 8:19 NASB, emphasis mine)

If you read commentaries on Daniel, you will most likely find they say this vision in chapter 8 relates to the Persians and the Greeks. But it does not. The vision in Daniel 8 is a prophecy for the time immediately before Jesus's return. This is highly significant.

DANIEL 8 IS PROPHECY FOR OUR TIME.

Most likely, the "time of the end" referenced in this vision began when Jesus's first sign was fulfilled when Israel became a nation (in 1948).

That would mean we are currently in this period, and this prophecy could be fulfilled at any time.

In Daniel 8, the prophet saw a ram and a goat. The angel Gabriel tells Daniel what these animals represent. Remember, he also told Daniel this vision "applied to the time of the end," not to ancient times. So when Gabriel mentions the name of a nation to Daniel, its identity will be the modern nation that is located where the ancient nation mentioned was located. The names Turkey and Iran would have meant nothing to Daniel, so the angel gave him ancient names. The angel told Daniel:

> The ram which you saw with the two horns represents the kings of Media and Persia. The shaggy goat represents the kingdom of Greece. (Daniel 8:20–21 NASB)

Media and Persia were ancient kingdoms in the area now controlled by Iran. So the ram is Iran. We are told the goat is Greece. The Hebrew word translated "Greece is" *Yavan.* Yavan were an ancient people who occupied eastern Greece and western Turkey, including the city Istanbul. Istanbul is the prominent city in that region and was also the seat of power of the former Ottoman Empire, or caliphate, that ruled the Middle East for five hundred years. So, although our translations say Greece, the angel is telling Daniel that Turkey will be the goat.

The fact that the angel Gabriel used these ancient names (Media, Persia, and Yavan) has been a stumbling block to many for thousands of years. Let's review again why this vision refers only to modern nations. First, Gabriel tells us the vision applies to "the time of the end." He mentions this twice as if for emphasis. Second, the historic foreshadowing events were not a perfect match with the prophecy. For both of these reasons we know the ram is Iran and the goat is Turkey.

Now, let's first look at what happens to Iran in this vision. We are viewing the very near future when we read this. Remember, God has given us this vision so we can anticipate the coming of the Antichrist, the tribulation, and the return of his Son.

I looked in the vision, and while I was looking I was in the citadel of Susa, which is in the province of Elam; and I looked in the vision and I myself was beside the Ulai Canal. Then I lifted my eyes and looked, and behold, a ram which had two horns was standing in front of the canal. Now the two horns were long, but one was longer than the other, with the longer one coming up last. I saw the ram butting westward, northward, and southward, and no other beasts could stand before him nor was there anyone to rescue from his power, but he did as he pleased and magnified himself. (Daniel 8:2–4 NASB)

First, we notice Daniel is in a real, historic location. He mentions the ancient city of Susa and the Ulai Canal.

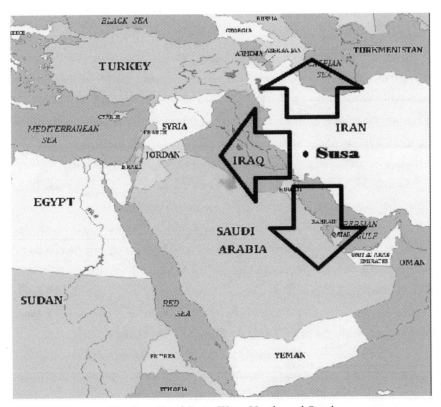

The Ram Head Butts West, North, and South

This map is of modern Iran and the Middle East but shows the location of ancient Susa. The Ulai Canal is based on a Hebrew word, so we are not completely sure where it was. Most historians believe it was a canal connecting two rivers in the near vicinity of Susa.

We are then told the ram (Iran) head butts his way from Susa westward, northward, and southward.

IRAN IS GOING TO INVADE THE MIDDLE EAST!

What countries might Iran invade? West and north of Susa (where the ram is located) are Iraq and Syria. South of Susa is the Arabian Peninsula. This prophecy is as fresh and timely as today's CNN report. I am writing this chapter in 2014. The Islamic State (ISIS) has entered and conquered the northern half of Iraq and eastern Syria. Both of these nations had been recently aligned with Iran. It is entirely conceivable that Iran will invade these territories to oust the Islamic State. Saudi Arabia is a traditional enemy of Iran as well. It is also possible that Iran may invade Saudi Arabia in response to Saudi Arabia's artificial price reduction in oil. This price reduction has been crippling to the Iranian economy.

Might an Iranian invasion of the Middle East affect the distribution of oil and worldwide economies? Indeed, it might.

Daniel's vision also tells us that "no other beasts could stand before him nor was there anyone to rescue from his power, but he did as he pleased." This means Iran will invade the Middle East unopposed. The United States and Europe will not stop Iran. Why won't the Western nations stop Iran? There are several possibilities. First, it is possible they will be too war-weary to fight. Or they may have experienced economic collapse and be unable to afford to fight. Iran's nuclear capability may be established, and they may be unwilling to fight a nuclear power. It is also possible the Western powers will align with Iran. You may be thinking that is impossible, but the enemy of my enemy is my friend. Western powers may align with Iran to destroy the terrorist Islamic State. We don't know the reason why the Western nations don't stop Iran's aggression. We just know that no one stops them, and Iran becomes great.

Iran follows the Shia sect of Islam. The Islamic State, Turkey, and Saudi Arabia are Sunni Muslims. For fourteen hundred years there has been great animosity between Shias and Sunnis—the conflict is over which descendants of Mohammad are to lead the Islamic faith. Animosity between these two groups has been fierce and will continue to be so. Remember the angel's words to Hagar, Abraham's Egyptian wife, related to her son, Ishmael, "He will be a wild donkey of a man; his hand will be against everyone and everyone's hand against him, and he will live in hostility toward all his brothers" (Genesis 16:12 NIV). We see this playing out even today in the Middle East.

Might the fact that Iran is going to become great mean that Iran forms a second caliphate, a Shia-based caliphate, to replace the Islamic State's current one? It might. Even if it doesn't, Turkey will not be pleased that a Shia Muslim state has become great.

Let's see what God's Word says will happen next.

> While I was observing, behold, a male goat was coming from the west over the surface of the whole earth without touching the ground; and the goat had a conspicuous horn between his eyes. He came up to the ram that had the two horns, which I had seen standing in front of the canal, and rushed at him in his mighty wrath. I saw him come beside the ram, and he was enraged at him; and he struck the ram and shattered his two horns, and the ram had no strength to withstand him. So he hurled him to the ground and trampled on him, and there was none to rescue the ram from his power. Then the male goat magnified himself exceedingly. (Daniel 8:5–8 NASB)

The goat (Turkey) will strike the ram (Iran) with mighty wrath. We are told the goat is enraged at the ram. Why would Turkey hate Iran? They will be enraged because Iran is Shia while Turkey is largely Sunni. That's all the reason they need. God's Word tells us a war will break out between the Shia and Sunni Muslims.

TURKEY WILL CRUSH IRAN AND BECOME *EXCEEDINGLY* GREAT.

Does this mean the creation of yet a third caliphate based in Turkey? Again, it might. If you are interested in learning even more about this vision in Daniel 8, purchase the book *Daniel Revisited* (WestBow, 2013) by Mark Davidson.

The goat (Turkey) is led by a leader the Bible refers to as the "conspicuous horn." We are told this leader "magnified himself exceedingly." Turkey will have conquered most of the Middle East at this point. Might this leader declare himself caliph, leader of the Muslim world, at that point? We don't know. What we do know is this leader is removed from power not long after winning the Sunni-Shia War. God's Word says the "large horn was broken." This may mean he dies or is removed from office. We aren't sure why he loses his power. We just know he does.

> But as soon as he was mighty, the large horn was broken; and in its place there came up four conspicuous horns toward the four winds of heaven. *Out of one of them came forth a rather small horn* which grew exceedingly great toward the south, toward the east, and toward the Beautiful Land. It grew up to the host of heaven and caused some of the host and some of the stars to fall to the earth, and it trampled them down. It even magnified itself to be equal with the Commander of the host; and it removed the regular sacrifice from Him, and the place of His sanctuary was thrown down. (Daniel 8:8–11 NASB, emphasis mine)

> ## THE SUNNI-SHIA WAR LAUNCHES THE
> ## REIGN OF THE ANTICHRIST.

This prophecy has enormous spiritual implications. Not only is it the prophecy that leads to the rise of the Antichrist, it is likely to be fulfilled in our lifetimes, if not within the next months or years. As such it will give the Church an unprecedented opportunity to practice apocalyptic evangelism as discussed in chapter four. It is an easily identified prophecy that will be fulfilled in the sight of the whole world. Millions may be brought to faith if this prophecy and its soon fulfillment are utilized in the way Peter used Joel 2 in chapter four.

> ## THE FULFILLED PROPHECY OF DANIEL 8 MAY
> ## GIVE THE CHURCH ITS SINGLE GREATEST
> ## EVANGELISTIC OPPORTUNITY OF ALL TIME.

In the preceding passage, the Antichrist is known as the "small horn." In most translations he is called the "little horn." We see, upon the "breaking of the large horn" (Turkey's leader), that the new empire which Turkey just formed from the majority of the Middle East is divided into four nations. Scripture tells us the Antichrist (the little horn) will arise from one of these nations.

How might Christians react to this war? Might they be scared that the end has come? Is this why Jesus tells us in Matthew 24 not to be frightened?

> You will be hearing of wars and rumors of wars. *See that you are not frightened*, for those things must take place, but that is not yet the end. For nation will rise against nation, and kingdom against kingdom. (Matthew 24:6–7 NASB, emphasis mine)

I believe Jesus could only be referring to prophesied wars in this passage, as war is common and has occurred throughout history. For Jesus's words to be a sign, he must be referring to specific wars prophesied to happen prior to his return. He also expects Christians to normally be frightened by this war. That is why he specifically tells us not to be frightened.

This is a major reason Jesus has instructed us to watch the "beginning of the birth pains" by saying "be observant" (Gk: *blepete*) in Matthew 24:4. He wants his bride to know the signs leading up to the revealing of the Antichrist, and he doesn't want us to be frightened. He wants us to know he is in control.

GENERIC OR SPECIFIC VIEW

Saying that Jesus could only be referring to prophesied wars flies in the face of another traditional belief. Nearly every Bible commentator I have ever read has considered the signs in the "beginning of the birth pangs" (Matthew 24:4–8) to be generic. Some take a long-term view and say that the world has always been beset by war, famine, and earthquakes. They claim that these general conditions are the signs Jesus spoke of. Others take a short-term view and believe that Jesus was speaking of events that will occur right before his return, but they still assume these events will be a general rise in the level of war, famine, and earthquakes.

But if the beginnings of the birth pangs are to be signs, doesn't it make sense that they will occur close to Jesus's return? Labor pains don't occur over a period of months in a pregnancy. They occur in a concentrated period at the very end. Also, doesn't it make sense that if they are signs, they will be specific? Isn't it likely that they will be events prophesied elsewhere in scripture, rather than being generic?

Christopher Mantei of Voice of the Martyrs ministry organization has done a wonderful study that shows that Jesus's use of the words "kingdom against kingdom" in the beginning of the birth pangs is a direct quote from Isaiah. It is incredibly likely that Jesus in the Olivet Discourse was making a specific reference to these quoted events by referencing this passage:

> Behold, the Lord is riding on a swift cloud and is about to come to Egypt; the idols of Egypt will tremble at His presence, and the heart of the Egyptians will melt within them. "So I will incite Egyptians against Egyptians; and they will each fight against his brother and each against his neighbor, city against city and *kingdom against kingdom*." (Isaiah 19:1–2 NASB, emphasis mine)

This prophecy is obviously related to the return of Jesus ("the Lord is riding on a swift cloud"), and it also details a civil war in Egypt that occurs around that time. This civil war is initially neighbor against neighbor and city against city, but it expands into a war between kingdoms. The passage continues:

> "Moreover, I will deliver the Egyptians into the hand of a cruel master, and a mighty king will rule over them," declares the Lord God of hosts. (Isaiah 19:4 NASB)

Most consider this cruel master who is a mighty king to be the Antichrist. In Daniel we find another passage that speaks of the Antichrist and a war with Egypt.

> At the end time the king of the South will collide with him [the Antichrist], and the king of the North [the Antichrist] will storm against him [the King of the South] . . . Then he will stretch out his [Antichrist's] hand against other countries,

and the land of Egypt will not escape. But he will gain control over the hidden treasures of gold and silver and over all the precious things of Egypt. (Daniel 11:40, 42–43 NASB, clarification mine)

Interestingly, when the kingdom of Alexander the Great was divided into four sub-kingdoms at his death, the two most powerful were based in two countries—Egypt (the king of the South) and in Assyria (the king of the North). In a previous section we noted that the Antichrist will be Assyrian. The war between these ancient kingdoms (Egypt and Assyria) was a foreshadow of the war that will occur in the future between the Antichrist from Assyria and Egypt. Was Jesus referring to this specific war when he said "kingdom against kingdom"? It is incredibly likely.

In fact, it is probable Jesus was specifically referring to both the Great Sunni-Shia War of Daniel 8 and the war between the Antichrist and Egypt when he prophesied "wars" in the "beginning of the birth pangs."

Not Roman and Not Antiochus

Before we delve further into this vision, we should probably pause here to answer two nagging questions you might have. *Isn't the Antichrist supposed to be Roman or at least European? And isn't the little horn supposed to be Antiochus Epiphanies, a historic king of Syria?*

We know the Antichrist is *not* Roman because this passage we have just studied shows that he arises from a Middle Eastern nation. This is consistent with the passages we saw in Micah and Isaiah that show he will be Assyrian and the passage in 1 John that suggests he may be Muslim.

Historically, Christians have believed he would be Roman because of two passages in the book of Daniel. However, instead of supporting a Roman Antichrist, these passages support the fact he will be Islamic. Let's see why that is so.

The first passage is the famous dream (found in Daniel 2) of King Nebuchadnezzar that was interpreted by Daniel. Nebuchadnezzar's dream was of a statue made out of the following four metals: gold, silver, bronze, and iron. These represented kingdoms that would rule Babylon. A fifth kingdom, the toes of the statue, was of iron and clay mixed. At the end of the dream, a rock not hewn by human hands (representing Jesus) destroyed the statue and set up an everlasting kingdom (the rock grows into a mountain that covers the whole earth). Essentially, the dream (given to Nebuchadnezzar by God and interpreted by God) shows the history of the world from the perspective of Babylon.

The fourth kingdom of this dream, the "legs of iron," is not identified. Historically, Christians have believed it was Rome. Joel Richardson, in his book *Mideast Beast* (WND 2012), uses Daniel 2:40 to clearly show the fourth kingdom is not Rome, but Islam.

> Then there will be a fourth kingdom as strong as iron; inasmuch as iron *crushes* and shatters all things, so, like iron that breaks in pieces, it will crush and break all these in pieces. (Daniel 2:40 NASB, emphasis mine)

The key word in this verse is "crushes." Richardson shows that only Islam crushed the culture, language, and religions of their conquered nations to make a homogenous Islamic land. Rome allowed foreign religions and languages to flourish in their territories. They did not crush the culture of these nations. In fact, Rome adopted Greek as the language of business throughout the empire. Additionally, the verse above says the fourth kingdom would crush the previous three kingdoms. Rome never conquered Persia (the second kingdom), and they conquered and held Babylon (the first kingdom) for only one year. Conversely, Islam conquered these parts of the world and still controls them today, and literally crushed the conquered nations' cultures, which is distinctive of Islam. For all these reasons, Islam, not Rome, is the fourth kingdom of Nebuchadnezzar's dream.

Interestingly, in Arabic this verb "crush" is *daesh*. It can also mean to trample underfoot. The acronym name of the current Islamic State

(ISIS or ISIL) in Muslim countries is "Daesh."[25] This takes on huge prophetic meaning when considering this passage from Daniel that discusses the empire of the Beast.

> I kept looking in the night visions, and behold, a fourth beast, dreadful and terrifying and extremely strong; and it had large iron teeth. It devoured and *crushed* and *trampled down the remainder with its feet.* (Daniel 7:7 NASB, emphasis mine)

THE PEOPLE OF THE PRINCE TO COME

Other historic interpretations look to Daniel 9:26 as proof that the Antichrist will come out of Rome.

> The people of the prince who is to come [the Antichrist] will destroy the city and the sanctuary. (Daniel 9:26 NASB, clarification mine)

The Roman legions destroyed Jerusalem and the temple in AD 70. Most commentators then assumed this meant the Antichrist would be Roman. However, two arguments dispute this. First, it is not entirely clear that Daniel 9:26 is referring to the past or to a future destruction of the temple and the city. Second, and more importantly, Richardson and Davidson have shown in their previously referenced books how the Roman legions that destroyed the temple were composed of numerous Arabs and Syrians. If this passage is historic, it supports an Islamic Antichrist more than a Roman one, since it was the Syrian soldiers who destroyed the temple. The best reference of all on this matter is the book *The Coming Bible Prophecy Reformation* by Rodrigo Silva (CreateSpace Independent Publishing Platform, 2014). If you enjoy reading the original historic texts, this book presents a treasure trove of writings about the ancient Roman army that besieged Jerusalem.

Many Christian interpreters also assume the little horn in Daniel 8 is Antiochus IV of the Seleucid Empire. Antiochus was never a little horn, a minor political figure who rises to power. Antiochus was the son of the king and rose to power through natural succession. Second, the verse in Daniel 8 says the little horn causes the stars (angels) to be cast down and tries to make himself equal with Christ. These are not things Antiochus accomplished. The little horn in this passage definitively refers to the Antichrist of our near future and not Antiochus.

SEVEN KINGDOMS

The concept that the Antichrist and his empire will be Islamic may be new to you. It is important to understand this point, because we won't see the Antichrist coming if we don't know where to look.

Revelation 17 gives us further understanding of the Islamic connection to the return of Jesus. In that chapter, an angel of God tells John that there will be seven heads on a beast that comes up out of the abyss. This passage in Revelation chapter 17 is quite strange and has been misunderstood.

> The beast that you saw was, and is not, and is about to come up out of the abyss and go to destruction. And those who dwell on the earth, whose name has not been written in the book of life from the foundation of the world, will wonder when they see the beast that he was and is not and will come. Here is the mind which has wisdom. *The seven heads are seven mountains*, on which the woman sits, *and they are seven kings*; five have fallen, one is, the other has not yet come; and when he comes, he must remain a little while. *The beast which was and is not, is himself also an eighth and is one of the seven*, and he goes to destruction. (Revelation 17:8–11 NASB, emphasis mine)

We notice these seven heads are seven mountains and seven kings. We saw in Daniel 2 that "mountain" is a symbol for kingdom, so the seven heads are seven kingdoms and seven kings. In a vain attempt to make this passage about Rome, traditional interpretations claim the seven heads are seven hills (Rome), not mountains. The Greek word translated "mountain," however, means a high mountain, not the rolling hills of Rome.

We have seen that there will be seven kingdoms. Most theologians believe these are the seven kingdoms that Satan has used throughout history to attempt to thwart God's plan of redemption. If that is true, those kingdoms would be:

Kingdom	Actions Taken to Thwart God's Plan of Redemption	Who Replaced Them
1.) Egypt	Pharaoh attempted genocide by killing Jewish baby boys by throwing them in the Nile.	Assyria conquered Egypt in 701 BC (Isaiah 20:1–6).
2.) Assyria	Conquered Israel and sent it into captivity, and nearly conquered Judah.	Babylon conquered Assyria in 612 BC.
3.) Babylon	Conquered Judah and took them into captivity.	Medes and Persians conquered Babylon in 539 BC (Daniel 5).
4.) Persia	Haman, in the Persian Court, attempted genocide of the Jews.	Greece conquered Persia in 324 BC.
5.) Greece	Antiochus IV desecrated the temple and killed thousands of Jews who would not convert to paganism.	Rome conquered Greece (the Seleucid Empire) in 64 BC.
6.) Rome	Rome crucified Jesus, killed Peter and Paul, killed numerous Christian martyrs, burned the temple and Jerusalem in AD 70, and sent the Jews into captivity.	Islam (the Ottoman Empire) conquered Rome in AD 1453.
7.) Islamic Caliphate	Killed millions of Jews and Christians during empire-building jihads. Crushed the nations where Christianity began, converting them to Islam. Built the Dome of the Rock on the Temple Mount in Jerusalem.	The Allies divided the Ottoman Empire after WWI (1924).

The Seven Kingdoms

From this table you can see that an unbroken stream of empires has been used by Satan to try to destroy Jews and Christians (God's people), and God's plan to redeem the world. One empire conquered another and replaced the former. As each new empire emerged, it became Satan's main strategic vehicle in his plan. These empires are the seven heads of the Beast. The line of these empires was unbroken for nearly four thousand years until 1924, after WWI when the Allied powers broke up the Ottoman Empire. In that year the Beast received a fatal head wound (one of its seven heads was cut off) and Satan no longer had an empire on the earth. We see evidence of this wound in Revelation 13:3 (NASB): "I saw one of his heads as if it had been slain, and his fatal wound was healed." With this understanding, this fatal head wound of the Beast has already happened, unlike most commentators' expectation that this will happen in the future to the actual Antichrist. This also is a key understanding.

Revelation 17 also gives testimony to this fatal wound by referring to the Beast that "was, and is not, and is about to come up out of the abyss." This implies two things. First, that these empires had a demonic component, because the beast comes out of the abyss, which is a holding area for demons. Second, it implies there was a period of time the Beast was not on the earth (is not). From Revelation 13:3 we learn that the head that received the fatal head wound is healed. That head was the Ottoman Empire. From this we can deduce the Ottoman Caliphate will be revived as the Beast Empire of Revelation 13.

> THE REVIVED OTTOMAN CALIPHATE WILL
> BE THE EMPIRE OF THE BEAST.

Events Leading to the Rise of Antichrist

Now that we know that the Antichrist will be Islamic, and we know his empire will be a revived Ottoman Empire, let us look at additional verses from the vision in Daniel 8 as they relate to the rise and identification of the Antichrist.

> A king will arise, insolent and skilled in intrigue. His power will be mighty, but not by his own power, and he will destroy to an extraordinary degree and prosper and perform his will; he will destroy mighty men and the holy people. And through his shrewdness he will cause deceit to succeed by his influence; and he will magnify himself in his heart, and he will destroy many while they are at ease. He will even oppose the Prince of princes, but he will be broken without human agency. (Daniel 8:23–25 NASB)

From these verses we learn the following character traits of the Antichrist:

- He is insolent.
- He is skilled in intrigue.
- He is shrewd.

We also see some of his accomplishments:

- He will destroy to an extraordinary degree.
- He will prosper.
- He will destroy mighty men, the holy people, and many at ease.
- He will oppose even Jesus.
- He will magnify himself.
- He will cause deceit to succeed.

From these verses we should expect a prideful, deceitful manipulator. Once he comes to power he will destroy and attack the unsuspecting. The Bible says he will "destroy to an extraordinary degree." What this entails we can only imagine, but it will be horrible.

But our Lord will destroy him (without human agency) with the breath of his mouth and the brightness of his appearing! Praise God!

OTHER SIGNS

It is possible that the additional signs (other than war) found in the beginning of the birth pangs in Matthew and Luke will accompany or possibly follow the great Sunni-Shia war and the rise of the Antichrist prophesied by Daniel. These signs are deception by false messiahs, a falling away from the faith of many Christians, famines, earthquakes, rebellions, plagues, terrors, and signs in the heavens. How these will play out or be connected to the war and the Antichrist, we can only guess. We have to watch to know.

The upcoming blood moon tetrad is a series of four lunar eclipses in a two-year period, all falling on Jewish feast days; this unusual phenomena is described in the book by Mark Biltz, *Blood Moons* (WND Books, 2014). This specific sign has occurred several other times in history. Might the blood moon tetrad that is occurring in 2014–2015 be one of the signs in the heavens? It might be. Previous similar eclipses occurred in the year Israel won its war of independence in 1949–1950, and in the year Jerusalem was freed in 1967–1968. The symmetry of this particular sign in 2014–2015 is astounding. No previous tetrad also included two solar eclipses on Jewish feast days in addition to the four lunar eclipses, which will be the case in 2015.

We have already shown the upcoming blood moon tetrad is not the prophesied celestial/earthly disturbance, but might it be a heavenly sign? The rise of the Islamic State caliphate occurred within two months of the first blood moon eclipse in this series. Also a minor war occurred between Israel and Hamas. The tetrad may be a precursor to the great Sunni-Shia war that is prophesied to come or an Israeli-Arab war. We will need to watch to know.

The word translated "earthquakes" in Matthew, Mark, and Luke is the Greek word *seismos* that means a literal shaking. *Seismos* may be an earthquake or any natural or man-made disaster. The storm on the Sea of Galilee that Jesus calmed was described as a *seismos*. A nuclear explosion would also classify as a *seismos*, so this is possibly what the scripture is speaking of. A nuclear blast is certainly a great shaking and a disaster. The Greek word translated "terrors" in Luke means a fearful sight that causes men to want to run away from it. This also could be a description of a nuclear explosion or a terror attack.

We need to be watchful for these signs. I am convinced that we will know they are signs from God when we see them. Please notice that I do not believe any of these signs are the wrath of God, rather they will be signs given by God prior to the day of the Lord, the period of God's wrath on the earth.

SIGNS DURING THE TRIBULATION

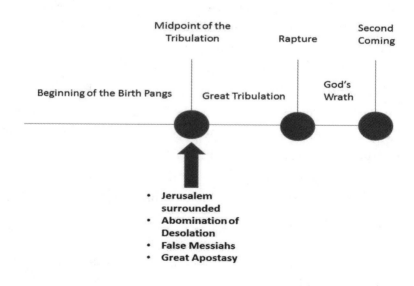

Signs during the Tribulation

The next series of signs that Jesus instructs us to watch for occur during the tribulation. We know from chapter two that the three main features of the tribulation period will be persecution, apostasy, and deliverance. These next signs will all exhibit these features to one extent or another. We also know the further out from the present we get, the less sure we are of details about a sign. This is true of these next four events. We know far less about them than the beginning of the birth pangs events. The four signs that occur during the great tribulation are:

- Events at the midpoint of the tribulation;
- False messiahs and lying signs;
- The great apostasy;
- Persecutions.

My understanding of scripture is that the events at the midpoint will come first and usher in the other signs for which Jesus wants us to look.

Events at the Midpoint of the Tribulation

Matthew and Mark mention the "abomination that causes desolation." Luke states that armies will surround Jerusalem. All three writers warn those in Judea to flee to the mountains when they see these events.

It is my opinion, this is the time when the Antichrist first invades Israel and surrounds Jerusalem. Luke records this event:

> But when you see Jerusalem surrounded by armies, then know that its desolation is near. Then let those who are in Judea flee to the mountains, let those who are in the midst of her depart, and let not those who are in the country enter her. *For these are the days of vengeance, that all things which are written may be fulfilled.* But woe to those who are pregnant and to those who are nursing babies in those days! For there will be great distress in the land and wrath upon this people. And they will fall by

the edge of the sword, and be led away captive into all nations. And *Jerusalem will be trampled by Gentiles until the times of the Gentiles are fulfilled.* (Luke 21:20–24 NKJV, emphasis mine)

Many prophecy teachers wrongly assume this passage from Luke applies exclusively to the destruction of Jerusalem and the temple in 70 AD. It does not. Those events were a foreshadowing of what is to come. How can we be sure these are future events? First, notice the verse: "For these are the days of vengeance, that **all** things which are written may be fulfilled." Obviously all prophecy wasn't fulfilled in 70 AD.

Second, notice the exact parallelism of these three verses from Matthew, Mark, and Luke:

Therefore when you see the 'abomination of desolation', spoken of by Daniel the prophet, standing in the holy place (whoever reads, let him understand), then let those who are in Judea flee to the mountains. (Matthew 24:15–16 NKJV)

So when you see the 'abomination of desolation,' spoken of by Daniel the prophet, standing where it ought not (let the reader understand), then let those who are in Judea flee to the mountains. (Mark 13:14 NKJV)

But when you see Jerusalem surrounded by armies, then know that *its desolation* is near. Then let those who are in Judea flee to the mountains. (Luke 21:20–21 NKJV, emphasis mine)

All three verses speak of the desolation of Jerusalem and fleeing to the mountains. Luke simply gives an earlier look at what will be a singular event: the capture of Jerusalem and the setting up of the abomination of desolation ("its desolation").

Third, if the events in Luke truly were in regard to 70 AD, Jesus was giving his followers seemingly terrible advice. The Roman armies slowly approached Jerusalem starting in 66 AD. By the time they encircled the city, it was essentially too late to escape. Many were slaughtered at this time trying to slip through the Roman lines.

Now that we see that Luke 21 verses 20–21 and, by extension, Luke 21 verses 23–24 are future, let's carefully look at what they prophesize. It clearly states that many will die in the siege of Jerusalem and that many will be taken as captives into all the nations. This imprisonment of the Jews (and Jesus's subsequent setting the captives free) is found in numerous scriptures: Psalm 14:7; Psalm 102:13, 19, 20; Isaiah 11:11–12,15–16; Isaiah 27:12–13; Isaiah 35:5–6; Isaiah 42:6–7, 16; Isaiah 52:11–12; Isaiah 61:1–3; Jeremiah 31:8–10; Ezekiel 39:25–28; Joel 2:32–3:1; Hosea 11:11; Micah 2:12–13; Micah 4:6–7; Micah 5:6; Micah 7:12; and Zechariah 10:6–11.

As Christians, if we anticipate this horrible atrocity, what should we be doing now to prepare? In chapter seven, we discuss the specific steps that our Lord has given us to prepare. Jesus has not left us to our own imaginations. He has given us precise instructions.

THE TIMES OF THE GENTILES

Luke 21:24 concludes by saying that Jerusalem will be trampled until the "times of the Gentiles" are complete. What does the times of the Gentiles mean? Is it the entire time from 70 AD until the present, or is it the three-and-a-half years that the Antichrist and his empire control Jerusalem?

The Greek word translated "times" is *kairos*, which means "appointed time." This is the same word used in the Septuagint translation of Daniel 7:25 for "time, times and half a time," which is known to mean the final 42-month reign of the Antichrist. Revelation makes it clear that the trampling of the city will be this three-and-a-half-year period:

> But leave out the court which is outside the temple, and do not measure it, for it has been given to the Gentiles. And they will *tread* the holy city underfoot for *forty-two months* [three-and-a-half years]. (Revelation 11:2 NKJV, emphasis and clarification mine)

Isaiah poetically describes this period:

> So now let Me tell you what I am going to do to My vineyard: I will remove its hedge and it will be consumed; I will break down its wall and it will become *trampled* ground. I will lay it waste; It will not be pruned or hoed, But *briars and thorns* will come up. I will also charge the clouds to *rain no rain* on it. (Isaiah 5:5–6 NASB, emphasis mine)

Notice this also refers to the trampling, and "briars and thorns" (the Gentile nations) growing up within Israel. Jerusalem falls because God removes his hedge of protection. Of greatest interest to me is the final line that says no rain will fall. Is this part of the mission of the Two Witnesses?

> "These have the power to shut up the sky, so that rain will not fall during the days of their prophesying; and they have power over the waters to turn them into blood, and to strike the earth with every plague, as often as they desire." (Revelation 11:6 NASB)

After the capture of Jerusalem, the Antichrist is ready for his defining moment as explained below.

THE ABOMINATION OF DESOLATION

When the Antichrist enters the temple of God, he will proclaim himself to be God. This accompanies the abomination that causes desolation. Let us look at this verse again.

> Therefore when you see the ABOMINATION OF DESOLATION, spoken of by Daniel the prophet, standing in the holy place (whoever reads, let him understand), then let those who are in Judea flee to the mountains. (Matthew 24:15–16 NKJV)

Notice these verses say the abomination will *stand* in the holy place. Paul in 2 Thessalonians says the Man of Sin (the Antichrist) will *sit* in the temple of God. The abomination may be the man or something else. Matthew, the writer of the book of Matthew, specifically enters a parenthetical warning into Jesus's direct quote to alert his readers: "Whoever reads, let him understand." This makes it clear that we are to attempt to understand this evil sign. In Revelation, we learn that an image of the beast is set up. Might this be the abomination?

> Telling those who dwell on the earth to make an *image to the beast* who was wounded by the sword and lived. He was granted power to give breath to the image of the beast, that the image of the beast should both speak and cause as many as would not worship the image of the beast to be killed. (Revelation 13:14–15 NKJV, emphasis mine)

THE IMAGE OF THE FIRST BEAST

This image of the beast reminds us of the golden statue King Nebuchadnezzar of Babylon set up, and of which he demanded be worshiped as described in Daniel:

> Nebuchadnezzar the king made an *image of gold*, the height of which was sixty cubits and its width six cubits; he set it up on the plain of Dura in the province of Babylon. . . . you are to fall down and worship the *golden image* that Nebuchadnezzar the king has set up." (Daniel 3:1, 5 NASB, emphasis mine)

In Daniel chapter 2, the account of Nebuchadnezzar's dream of a huge metal statue is given. When God helped Daniel interpret the dream, he informed Nebuchadnezzar that Babylon was the head of gold of the statue, and that other kingdoms, inferior to Babylon, would assume preeminence after Babylon's fall. Nebuchadnezzar didn't like what God revealed to him in his dream. He didn't want Babylon's kingdom to end, and he later made his own statue in defiance of God's revealed Word. Nebuchadnezzar's statue was all gold (the metal representing Babylon) rather than multiple metals. It was an *image* of Babylon. He was in essence saying to God, *You may have a statue of different metals and think other kingdoms will replace Babylon, but my statue is only gold. Babylon will last forever.*

In Daniel chapter 3, we learn more details about this statue, contained in the scripture quotation given just previously. This statue which Nebuchadnezzar set up is a foreshadowing of the final abomination. First of all, it is an image of the Beast. We know from Daniel 7 that four beasts will arise from the sea. Ancient Babylon was the first of the four beasts that Daniel prophesied. Gold was the color of the Babylonian portion of Nebuchadnezzar's statue in his dream, so an image of gold was an image of the first beast. We know from Revelation 13 that the final abomination will be an image of the fourth Beast, the final Beast.

We also see 60 and 6 given as measurements of Nebuchadnezzar's golden statue in Daniel 3:1. We, similarly, know from Revelation 13:18 that the number of the final Beast will be 600, 60, and 6 ("666"). It seems like God's Word is telling us that this ancient image from Babylon is like the final one that is to come, but it is not evil to quite the same extreme as the final version (66 versus 666).

After the image was set up, Nebuchadnezzar commanded everyone to bow to the image, just as the False Prophet will command everyone to bow to the image of the fourth Beast. In the Septuagint Old Testament, the Greek word for "bow down" found in Daniel 3 is *proskuneó,* which is the identical Greek word translated in Revelation as "worship" in the following passage about the final abomination of desolation:

> And it was given to him to give breath to the *image of the beast,* so that the image of the beast would even speak and cause as many as do not *worship* the image of the beast to be killed. (Revelation 13:15 NASB, emphasis mine)

This Greek word literally means "to kiss the ground in reverence to something greater." This is a perfect picture of how Muslims bow to Mecca. We also see in Daniel 3 that Nebuchadnezzar ordered a call to worship to be played by an orchestra of instruments. It was upon that signal that the bowing was to take place. This is also a perfect picture of the Muslim "call to prayer" that plays from their minarets prior to each of these prayer sessions.

The Image of the Fourth Beast

At this point, we do not know exactly what the abomination will be. Anyone who says they know what it will be is only guessing. That is why we are to watch. Scripture, however, gives us tantalizing hints. Does an image of a false god have to be a statue? The book of Acts describes the image of the false Greek god Artemis that was possibly not a statue:

> The city clerk quieted the crowd and said: "Fellow Ephesians, doesn't all the world know that the city of Ephesus is the guardian of the temple of the great Artemis and of *her image, which fell from heaven*? (Acts 19:35 NIV, emphasis mine)

It is interesting to consider that this image might have been a black meteorite. There is a long history of the worship of meteorites in the Middle East.

In the *Apocrypha*, books of the Bible that are outside the accepted, inspired, canon of scripture, we find the story of the Jewish holiday Hanukkah. This story also provides a foreshadowing of the final abomination of desolation described by Jesus in his Olivet Discourse (Matthew 24:15). Antiochus Epiphanes (who we have discussed previously) set up this evil sign and desecrated the altar of burnt sacrifices in the temple. When the temple was later cleansed by the Jewish priests, the following passage describes the removal of the abomination:

> They cleansed the sanctuary and took the polluted *stones* to a ritually unclean place. (1 Mac. 4:42 CEB, emphasis mine)

Johnathan Goldstein has speculated that the stones that were removed were *meteorites* (*I Maccabees* [Garden City NY: Doubleday, 1976] Anchor Bible Series, p.149). He based his assumption on Daniel 8:10 where we see the "little horn" causing some of the "stars to fall to the earth." Might this be referring to meteorites? We can't know for sure.

What we are sure of, however, is that the most sacred object in Islam is a meteorite. The Black Stone is set within the walls of the Kaaba in Mecca, and it is worshiped by Muslims the world over. This is speculation on my part, but might this Black Stone, Islam's most holy object, be moved to the temple of God during the tribulation (Seventieth Week of Daniel)? Might it be the image of the Beast? It certainly represents Islam.

We have seen previously in Revelation 13:13–14 that the False Prophet will give breath to the Beast and it will speak. Muslims fully expect the Black Stone to speak prior to the Day of Judgment! The following Islamic hadith says of the Black Stone:

> Ibn `Abbas (may Allah be pleased with him) further related that the Prophet (peace and blessings be upon him) said: "By Allah, Allah will bring it forth on the Day of Judgment, and *it will have two eyes with which it will see and a tongue with which it will speak*, and it will testify in favor of those who touched it in sincerity." (At-Tirmidhi, Sunan, emphasis mine)

Daniel's vision of the little horn uses almost identical language:

> This horn possessed *eyes like the eyes of a man and a mouth* uttering great boasts. (Daniel 7:8 NASB, emphasis mine)

Is the Black Stone of the Kaaba the abomination of desolation? Only time will tell. Regardless of what the abomination turns out to be, setting up the abomination will signal the revealing of the Antichrist. Up to this point, we may suspect who he is. However, only by him sitting in the temple of God and setting up the abomination will we *know* who he is. This is an enormously critical point. We may suspect someone during the beginning of the birth pangs period, but we will not know for certain until this event takes place. Indeed, the confirmation of a peace treaty of the Antichrist "with many" (including Israel), which starts the Seventieth Week of Daniel (the tribulation), may be done in secret and may not be a public event to openly signal the identity of the Antichrist (Daniel 9:27). This peace treaty is a sign many are looking for, but Jesus himself does not mention it as a sign to be watched for.

> THE ABOMINATION OF DESOLATION IDENTIFIES THE ANTICHRIST AND IS THE SIGN THAT INTENSE PERSECUTION IS ABOUT TO BEGIN.

FALSE MESSIAHS AND LYING SIGNS

Jesus tells us false messiahs will arise and even claim to be Jesus himself.

> Take heed that no one deceives you. For many will come in My name, saying, "I am the Christ," and will deceive many . . . Then if anyone says to you, "Look, here is the Christ!" or "There!" do not believe it. For false Christs and false prophets will rise and show great signs and wonders to deceive, if possible, even the elect. *See, I have told you beforehand.* Therefore if they say to you, "Look, He is in the desert!" do not go out; or "Look, He is in the inner rooms!" do not believe it. (Matthew 24:4–5, 23–26 NKJV, emphasis mine)

This is Jesus's most stern warning in the entire Olivet Discourse. He first says the False Messiah and False Prophet will show great signs that could deceive the elect in Christ (if possible). He then emphasizes this by saying, "See, I have told you beforehand."

Muslim tradition teaches that a Jesus will return to the earth to help their messiah figure, the Mahdi. Their name for this false Jesus is Isa, son of Mary.[26] To the Muslims he will be a prophet, not the Son of God as described in the Bible. What a horrible deception it might be if a miracle-working Jesus arises, claiming to be Jesus Christ himself and denies that he is divine! What if he says he never was divine or never died on a cross! How many might be taken in by this deception?

Revelation appropriately calls this figure "False Prophet" (since Muslims consider Isa a prophet).

> He [the False Prophet] exercises all the authority of the first beast in his presence, and causes the earth and those who dwell in it *to worship the first beast,* whose deadly wound was healed. He *performs great signs, so that he even makes fire come down from heaven* on the earth in the sight of men. And he deceives those who dwell on the earth by those signs which he was granted to do in the sight of the beast, telling those who dwell on the earth to *make an image to the beast* who was wounded by the sword and lived. He was granted power to give breath to the image of the beast, that the image of the beast should both speak and cause as many as would not worship the image of the beast to be killed. He causes all, both small and great, rich and poor, free and slave, *to receive a mark on their right hand or on their foreheads,* and that no one may buy or sell except one who has the mark or the name of the beast, or the number of his name. (Revelation 13:12–17 NKJV, clarification and emphasis mine)

We see by this the False Prophet has four main missions:

- To cause the world to worship the Beast;

- To perform great lying signs;

- To make the image of the Beast and cause it to speak;

- To cause all men to receive the "mark of the Beast."

We also know from Muslim tradition that the False Prophet, Isa, is the one who commands Jews and Christians to be killed if they do not convert to Islam. If you wish to learn more about these Muslim traditions, the book *The Islamic Antichrist* (WND Books, 2009) by Joel Richardson details the amazing inverse similarities between Muslim traditions and the revealed Word of God.

What are the great signs that the Antichrist and the False Prophet will be given authority to do? It is suspected that the Antichrist *may* appear to be healed of a fatal head wound in his body just as the revived Ottoman Caliphate will be healed politically. We also see from Revelation that the False Prophet will be able to call down fire from heaven. Deception will be rampant.

THE EMERGENCE OF THE MUSLIM JESUS IS THE SIGN THAT THE GREAT APOSTASY IS ABOUT TO BEGIN.

WHAT IS *THE* SIGN OF JESUS'S RETURN?

Jesus commands us that we are not to go out to see this False Prophet if we hear about him in the "desert" or the "inner room" (the Holy of Holies in the temple?) Rather, Jesus commands us to watch for the sign to properly identify him as the real Jesus upon his return.

For just as the lightning comes from the east and flashes even to the west, so will the coming of the Son of Man be. Wherever the corpse is, there the vultures will gather. (Matthew 24:27–28 NASB)

This verse is incredibly important. In the previous verses Jesus had taught that the Antichrist and False Prophet would be allowed to perform signs that could mislead the elect if it were possible. They will not be allowed to duplicate the sign of the Shekinah glory of Jesus shining like lightning from the east to the west. As we just learned in chapter five, this verse also proves the resurrection and rapture occur at this point. It will not be a silent rapture! The entire world will see this sign.

THIS CRUCIAL SIGN WILL KEEP US FROM BEING LED ASTRAY.

As we learned in the previous chapter, God will dim the lights worldwide in a celestial/earthly disturbance, then will appear on the clouds in great glory, which is his Shekinah glory. This is the sign of his coming. All other signs of so-called messiahs are false.

Only God can produce this Shekinah glory. It first manifested in the Tent of Meeting and later in the temple of God in ancient Israel. In Ezekiel 10 and 11 we learn that Israel became so evil that the glory left the temple. In Luke 2:8–9 (NIV) we learn that the glory returned to earth upon the birth of Christ: "There were shepherds living out in the fields nearby, keeping watch over their flocks at night. An angel of the Lord appeared to them, and the glory of the Lord shone around them." In John 1:14 (NIV), John testified that he saw this glory on the Mount of Transfiguration, "We have seen his glory, the glory of the one and only Son, who came from the Father, full of grace and truth." Finally, that same glory is about to return to the earth upon the return of Christ. It is the sign we should look for to know it's him.

THE GREAT APOSTASY

After the Antichrist and False Prophet arise, they will seek to lead Christians astray. Jesus has told us:

> Take heed that no one deceives you. For many will come in my name, saying, 'I am the Christ,' and will deceive many. (Matthew 24:4–5 NKJV)

Many believe the great apostasy is occurring right now. However, what is happening now is more like the gradual apostasy. Certainly, liberal theology has chipped away at the base of Christianity, but what is happening now does not match Jesus's statement about the great falling away.

> At that time many will fall away and will betray one another and hate one another. Many false prophets will arise and will mislead many. Because lawlessness is increased, most people's love will grow cold. (Matthew 24:10–12 NASB)

We cannot say the love of most has grown cold at this time. The day is coming, however, when this will be true. What are the conditions that will lead to this falling away? The Bible mentions three factors:

- The mark of the Beast;
- Great persecution (tribulation);
- Lying signs and wonders.

It appears a "perfect storm" of these three factors will combine after the midpoint of the tribulation to cause the falling away from faith.

After the Antichrist invades Jerusalem and sits in the temple of God as if he were God, the False Prophet will institute an economic program where you will not be able to buy or sell without the mark of the Beast. Many will be unable to be self-sufficient and will give in to taking the mark in order to get food and shelter. The False Prophet will also cause all those to be killed who refuse to worship the Beast. Many will be unwilling to lay their lives down and will succumb to the worship of the Beast. Finally, to add validity to their policies, the Antichrist and False Prophet will perform signs that Jesus says will "mislead, if possible, even the elect." We looked at this three-part unholy ministry of the False Prophet in the last section.

Overcoming is the theme of Jesus's letters to the seven churches of Revelation. It will take an incredibly strong faith to overcome this witches' brew of deception and persecution. It will also take foreknowledge. Christians will need to know what to watch for so they are not led astray. This echoes Jesus's first command in the Olivet Discourse: "See to it [be observant] that no one misleads you" (Matthew 24:4 NASB, addition mine).

IF YOU ARE ASLEEP, YOU CAN'T BE OBSERVANT.

Perhaps, the most tragic aspect of the great falling away will be that some of our former brothers and sisters will betray us and even hate us. We can already see hatred against Christians and Jews growing. The world is redefining righteousness as intolerance and bigotry. The Bible tells us they will hate us and think they are doing God a favor.

The majority of churches believe their flocks will not experience the great apostasy, even though the Bible clearly states they will (2 Thessalonians 2:3). This is one effect of being asleep. This may also be why Jesus shows the door of heaven will be shut on half of the virgins in the parable we studied in chapter two. Jesus also said, "If the head of the house had known at what time of the night the thief was coming, he would have been on the alert and would not have allowed his house to be broken into." Jesus's teachings paint a clear, consistent, and sad picture of what is to come.

In chapter two we alluded to the parables in Matthew 24 and 25, where faithful churchgoers are described as being rewarded, and unfaithful churchgoers are described as being eternally separated from God. We also mentioned that these unfaithful churchgoers appear to be led astray in the great apostasy.

The clearest picture of the falling away of a churchgoer is the depiction of the evil slave found in the parable of the faithful and the evil slaves.

> But if that evil slave says in his heart, "My master is not coming for a long time," and begins to beat his fellow slaves and eat and drink with drunkards; the master of that slave will come on a day when he does not expect him and at an hour which he does not know, and will cut him in pieces and assign him a place with the hypocrites; in that place there will be weeping and gnashing of teeth. (Matthew 24:48–51 NASB)

As we mentioned in chapter two, we first see that this evil slave falls away because he is not watchful for the signs of Jesus's return. He says, "My master is not coming for a long time." He then undertakes two unusual acts: he beats his fellow slaves and eats and drinks with drunkards. Both of these acts indicate that this slave has fallen away as part of the great apostasy.

Beating of his fellow slaves is synonymous with Jesus's statement earlier in the Olivet Discourse that during the great apostasy: "Many will fall away and will betray one another and hate one another" (Matthew 24:10 NASB). However, eating and drinking with drunkards does not mean eating and drinking with those overcome by alcohol. Rather these are "those who dwell on the earth . . . made drunk with the wine of her [the great harlot's] immorality" (Revelation 17:2 NASB). We already have seen that the False Prophet will only allow those with the mark of the

Beast to buy or sell. Eating and drinking with those with the mark will be impossible for the godly. Only those who also take the mark will be able to buy and sell and thus eat and drink with drunkards. We can deduce from this that the evil slave has fallen away and taken the mark himself.

We must do everything possible to awaken the churches! Not only do we have to open the front door of our churches to welcome as many as possible to the wedding (see chapter four), but we also need to shut the back door so those who already know about Jesus are not lost. The number at risk is staggeringly large. We can offer up this prayer:

> Lord Jesus, your Word tells us we can do all things through Christ who strengthens us. Strengthen us for this mission. Help us awaken your Church. Amen.

PERSECUTION

Those who do not fall away will be subject to persecution. Jesus and Daniel do not mince words about how bad this will be.

> For then there will be a great tribulation, such as has not occurred since the beginning of the world until now, nor ever will. Unless those days had been cut short, no life would have been saved. (Matthew 24:21–22 NASB)

> Now at that time Michael, the great prince who stands guard over the sons of your people, will arise. And there will be a time of distress such as never occurred since there was a nation until that time. (Daniel 12:1 NASB)

We shudder to consider the Holocaust of WWII, but Jesus and Daniel say this will be much worse. That is why Jesus tells us, "Keep on the alert at all times, praying that you may have strength to escape all these things that are about to take place, and to stand before the Son of Man" (Luke 21:36 NASB).

Signs after the Great Tribulation

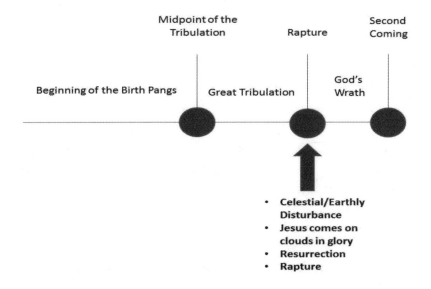

Signs after the Great Tribulation

In chapter five we looked at the celestial/earthly disturbance and the rapture. Both of these follow the great tribulation, which is cut short by the rapture. Immediately after the rapture, the day of the Lord (God's wrath) begins. Jesus does not mention this time in the Olivet Discourse because the saints will not see it. However, Revelation goes into considerable detail about God's wrath. The events known as the trumpet and bowl judgments describe the specifics of God's wrath.

Finally, at the end of the Olivet Discourse, Jesus gives us a glimpse of his judging the nations at the start of his kingdom before going into the millennium. We call this the prophecy of the goats, and the sheep judgment.

> But when the Son of Man comes in His glory, and all the angels with Him, then He will sit on His glorious throne. All the nations will be gathered before Him; and He will separate them from one another, as the shepherd separates the sheep

from the goats; and He will put the sheep on His right, and the goats on the left. (Matthew 25:31–33 NASB)

Christians who will be raptured are chosen based on the righteousness of Christ that is obtained through faith and trusting in him for salvation. In fact, all the dead, after the rapture, are later judged by their faith or lack of faith and trust in Jesus. So, who are these being judged by their works at the end of the tribulation? They must be the living survivors of the tribulation. They are those who were not Christians at the time of the rapture (or they would have been raptured) and at least didn't align with the Beast by taking his mark; they have lived through the period of God's wrath. Let's see how Jesus judges them.

> Then the King will say to those on His right, "Come, you who are blessed of my Father, inherit the kingdom prepared for you from the foundation of the world. For I was hungry, and you gave me something to eat; I was thirsty, and you gave me something to drink; I was a stranger, and you invited me in; naked, and you clothed me; I was sick, and you visited me; I was in prison, and you came to me." Then the righteous will answer him, "Lord, when did we see you hungry, and feed you, or thirsty, and give you something to drink? And when did we see you a stranger, and invite you in, or naked, and clothe you? When did we see you sick, or in prison, and come to you?" The King will answer and say to them, "*Truly I say to you, to the extent that you did it to one of these brothers of mine, even the least of them, you did it to me.*" (Matthew 25:34–40 NASB, emphasis mine)

So these living survivors of the tribulation are judged based on how they treated Christians and Jews ("the least of these my brothers") during the tribulation. Those who provide food, water, shelter, etc., will be allowed to enter God's kingdom in their normal human bodies (not with resurrection bodies like those who were raised and raptured); those who did not provide these essentials are considered as goats and are thrown into the lake of fire, along with the Antichrist and the False Prophet. Eventually, even these survivors who are allowed to enter Jesus's kingdom in their normal human bodies will die, and they will later be judged according to their faith at the great white throne judgment at the end of the millennium. But at this point, at the start of the millennium, they are allowed to live on into the millennium.

There is a lesson for us as well in this prophecy. When we see Christians or Jews suffering in the persecution, we are to help them in the same manner. In the next chapter we will examine this more closely. We should be aware that right now throughout the world much of the Church is already suffering. We should be providing for them right now as if they were Christ himself.

SUMMARY

In this chapter we have learned that Jesus gave the commands to watch or be observant over thirty times in the Olivet Discourse. It is his most emphatic and frequent command for his followers in regard to his return. We then learned the numerous events that will occur in each of the main sections of what have come to be known as the end times: the beginning of the birth pangs, the midpoint of the tribulation, the great tribulation, and the events after the tribulation.

The basic steps for getting ready for Jesus from this chapter are:

1. **We must know the signs of Jesus's return:**
   We should watch for signs to avoid persecution and deception.

2. **The sign Jesus gave that his return is near has already occurred:**
   The nation of Israel was recreated in 1948. The generation that saw Israel become a nation again is the final generation.

3. **The Antichrist and the Empire of the Beast will both be Islamic:**
   Christians deceived by this theory that the Antichrist will be European may miss seeing the Antichrist arise and may be unprepared and fall away from the faith.

4. **Daniel 8 foretells a war between Sunni and Shia Muslims:**
   This is most likely the next prophetic event on God's calendar and will lead to the rise of the Antichrist.

5. **The abomination of desolation identifies the Antichrist:**
   This evil sign will mark the beginning of the great tribulation.

6. **The Islamic Jesus, Isa, will be the False Prophet:**
   This sign will mark the beginning of the great apostasy.

7. **The sign of Jesus's return is his coming on the clouds in glory:**
   Knowing this sign will help Christians avoid deception.

In the next chapter we will examine the role that Israel will play in the last days, God's covenants with Israel, and the relationship of Christians and Jews.

CHAPTER SEVEN

SIBLING RIVALRY:

HOW TO RELATE TO ISRAEL

There is neither Jew nor Greek, there is neither slave nor free man, there is neither male nor female; for you are all one in Christ Jesus. (Gal. 3:28 NASB)

I attended college about two hours from the town where I grew up. The combination of a part-time job and studying didn't leave many weekends for visits home. But, a few times a semester, I'd throw my dirty laundry in my car and head back. (Why does every student think their mom would just *love* to do their laundry for them on home visits?) My favorite part of a visit home was ditching dorm food for a couple of home-cooked meals. I especially looked forward to my grandmother's apple fritters and potato pancakes. Sometime during my second semester, my grandmother stopped cooking the dishes I enjoyed and began substituting the one dish she made that I absolutely did not like. It was a Prussian dish made with ground hamburger and covered with a pastry. It doesn't sound all that bad, but it had the consistency and taste of cardboard.

Of course, I couldn't hurt her feelings and tell her I didn't like that dish. Instead I dutifully ate it on each visit. My grandmother would always say, "I know this is your favorite." I would tactfully tell her the dishes I really liked. After the second or third time she made this dish, I asked my mother if she would clue my grandmother in about what my true favorite dishes were. My mother was shocked. She said, "Your younger brother has been telling us all year what your favorite dishes are, and this one was at the top of the list." Well, it turns out my brother was telling my mom and grandmother all my *least* favorite foods. Based on my brother's recommendations, my mother and grandmother were stocking up on all the foods I didn't like for those special visits home. Now my brother knew full well what I liked and didn't like. This was his stealth approach at a practical joke. It worked because I remember it to this day. In fact, it worked too well. Until the day they died, both my mother and grandmother remembered my favorite dishes as the ones my brother told them, not my true favorites.

Did I deserve this treatment? Yes, and probably a whole lot more. Two brothers growing up in the same household get into a lot of mischief, especially in an unsaved household like ours. Sibling rivalry led to hundreds of similar harmless and not so harmless pranks over the years.

God's household is not much different. Romans 9:12 states, "The older will serve the younger." We Christians are the younger brother, and we have been telling tales about our older brother. Our older brother is Jacob, who of course is Israel, the Jewish people. If we are going to be ready for Jesus's return, we need to understand who our family members are and what Jesus has instructed us to do for them prior to his coming.

The first step is to stop telling lies about our brother. The most damaging tale we have been spreading about Israel is that God is finished with them. Many Christians believe the promises God gave to Israel now belong to the Church and that we are his new chosen people. You may have heard the Church referred to as God's New Israel. I read a book in college with that exact title.

The impact of this lie is enormous and leads directly to anti-Semitic and anti-Zionist prejudices. This philosophy fuels much of the anti-Israel sentiments that cause Christians to support the "poor Palestinian terrorists" as opposed to the Jews trying to protect their homes. It has also fueled much of the hatred behind Jewish persecutions throughout the age of the Church.

A second and related theological error that leads to anti-Semitism is the disbelief that God's kingdom will come in a physical form. These

Christians do not believe in a literal thousand-year kingdom on earth ruled by Jesus from Jerusalem. In combination, these theories lead Christians to view world events through lenses shaped by a secular media bias with no regard to history or the Bible.

What else would cause a self-professing Christian such as former President Jimmy Carter to raise funds for the Islamic Society of North America that has ties to the terrorist organization Hamas? No matter what your political opinions, your faith-based opinions would have to be skewed to even consider raising monies that ultimately fund groups like Hamas. You would have to believe the lie that Israel has no right to their land and that the Jews have no place in God's redemptive plan. Unfortunately, our former president is far from the only Christian supporting terrorists.[27]

You may also be asking, "Didn't the Church inherit God's promises to Israel? Or, didn't the Jews lose their rights to God's redemption by rejecting Jesus?" Let's look carefully at the answers because they dramatically affect how you view the world and how you view God himself.

God made numerous specific promises to Israel. If God has chosen to transfer those promises from Israel to the Church, what does that say about God's faithfulness, forgiveness, and grace? Obviously, the faithfulness of God precludes him reneging on his promises because of Israel's rejection. Once Israel repents, God's promises will be realized.

JESUS COMMENTS ON THE FUTURE OF ISRAEL

Obviously, Jesus must have something to say about the place of Israel after his return. In the book of Luke, Jesus makes two statements about the future of Israel. Both statements indicate there will be a period of time when Israel will reject him before his return. Jesus then discusses the restoration of Israel but clarifies it will not come *until* certain things happen.

> O Jerusalem, Jerusalem, the city that kills the prophets and stones those sent to her! How often I wanted to gather your

children together, just as a hen gathers her brood under her wings, and you would not have it! Behold, your house is left to you desolate; and I say to you, you will not see me *until* the time comes when you say, "Blessed is He who comes in the name of the Lord." (Luke 13:34–35 NASB, emphasis mine)

And they will fall by the edge of the sword, and will be led captive into all the nations; and Jerusalem will be trampled underfoot by the Gentiles *until* the times of the Gentiles are fulfilled. (Luke 21:24 NASB, emphasis mine)

Jesus does not say that Israel will be excluded, but rather that there will be a delay before they are included in his promises. Jesus does not indicate that Israel will not be part of his plan for redemption.

In Matthew, the disciples question their reward for giving up everything to follow Jesus. His response is that in the future, they will rule the twelve tribes of Israel.

And Jesus said to them [the apostles], "Truly I say to you, that you who have followed me, in the regeneration when the Son of Man will sit on His glorious throne, you also shall sit upon twelve thrones, judging the twelve tribes of *Israel.*" (Matthew 19:28 NASB, emphasis and clarification mine)

In Acts 1, we read how after Jesus had risen from the dead he spent the next forty days teaching and instructing his disciples. The disciples' final question for their master after this instruction is most revealing:

To these He also presented Himself alive after His suffering, by many convincing proofs, appearing to them over a period of forty days and speaking of the things concerning the kingdom of God. Gathering them together, He commanded them not to leave Jerusalem, but to wait for what the Father had promised, "Which," He said, "you heard of from Me; for

John baptized with water, but you will be baptized with the Holy Spirit not many days from now." So when they had come together, they were asking Him, saying, "Lord, is it at this time you are restoring the kingdom to Israel?" He said to them, "It is not for you to know times or epochs which the Father has fixed by His own authority; but you will receive power when the Holy Spirit has come upon you; and you shall be My witnesses both in Jerusalem, and in all Judea and Samaria, and even to the remotest part of the earth. (Acts 1:3–8 NASB)

I find it interesting that after forty days of intense instruction, Jesus didn't give them the slightest inkling that Israel was to be denied their promises or that the Church would replace them. We know this because the disciples didn't ask if the kingdom was to be restored to Israel, they asked if Jesus was going to do it right then and there. Jesus's response does not deny that the kingdom would be Israel's either. Rather, he says it is not for the disciples to know the timing. In regard to both the disciples and Jesus, it is not a question of *if* Israel's kingdom will be restored; it is a question of *when*.

GOD'S BELOVED

Romans chapters 9–11 are the primary texts that explain God's current relationship with Israel. I recommend you carefully read these chapters. We will start by looking at the place of the Church in God's plan.

I say then, they [the Jews] did not stumble so as to fall, did they? May it *never* be! But by their transgression salvation has come to the Gentiles, to make them [the Jews] jealous. (Romans 11:11 NASB, emphasis and clarifications mine)

Notice Paul tells us it was the transgression of the Jews (their rejecting Christ) that opened the door for our salvation. Does the special place that Christianity holds with God create jealousy among the Jews? Absolutely!

Paul then continues to show how the sin of the Jews (rejecting Jesus) made room for Gentiles.

> But if some of the branches were broken off, and you, being a wild olive, were grafted in among them and became partaker with them of the rich root of the olive tree, do not be arrogant toward the branches; but if you are arrogant, remember that it is not you who supports the root, but the root supports you. (Romans 11:17–18 NASB)

Many Christians have forgotten the essential truth that we are the ones who were grafted into the root of the Jewish tradition and a relationship to Christ. As Paul clearly demonstrates, it isn't the other way around. Also notice, only some of the branches were broken off to make room for us. What will happen someday to those branches that were broken?

> And they also, if they do not continue in their unbelief, will be grafted in, for God is able to graft them in again. For if you were cut off from what is by nature a wild olive tree, and were grafted contrary to nature into a cultivated olive tree, how much more will these who are the natural branches be grafted into their own olive tree? (Romans 11:23–24 NASB)

Paul makes it clear it is easier for the Jews to be grafted back in again than it is for Gentiles. This entire passage should fill us with humility at God's grace rather than conceit towards the Jews. Paul continues:

> For I do not want you, brethren, to be uninformed of this mystery—so that you will not be wise in your own estima-tion—that a partial hardening has happened to Israel until the fullness of the Gentiles has come in; and *so all Israel will be saved*; just as it is written, "The Deliverer will come from Zion, he will remove ungodliness from Jacob. This is my covenant

with them, when I take away their sins." (Romans 11:25–27 NASB, emphasis mine)

Did you know that one day all of Israel will be saved? The Bible clearly teaches this will happen after the "fullness of the Gentiles." One day the surviving remnant of the Jews will look upon their Messiah and cry out for forgiveness. The Old Testament prophets teach this.

> I will pour out on the house of David and on the inhabitants of Jerusalem, the Spirit of grace and of supplication, so that they will look on Me whom they have pierced; and they will mourn for Him, as one mourns for an only son, and they will weep bitterly over Him like the bitter weeping over a firstborn. (Zechariah 12:10 NASB)

> I will go away and return to My place [heaven] until they acknowledge their guilt and seek My face; in their affliction they will earnestly seek Me. (Hosea 5:15 NASB, clarification mine)

> "Come, let us return to the LORD for He has torn us, but He will heal us; He has wounded us, but He will bandage us. He will revive us after two days; He will raise us up on the third day, that we may live before Him." (Hosea 6:1–2 NASB)

The passage in Zechariah demonstrates the Jews will see the scars Jesus bears on his body from his time on the cross and repent. The passage in Hosea is fascinating. It clearly shows the Messiah returned to heaven, and he will remain there until the Jews acknowledge their guilt. This passage also hints at the timing of when the bodily return of Christ to the earth will take place. "He will revive us after two days" (after two thousand years); "He will raise us up on the third day" (in the Millennial Kingdom) "that we may live before Him" (commentary mine). We know that "with the Lord one day is like a thousand years" (2 Peter 3:8 NASB), so that time is fast approaching.

Paul concludes with a summary that explains our current relationship to the Jews and God's current relationship to them.

> From the standpoint of the gospel they are enemies for your sake, but from the standpoint of God's choice they are beloved for the sake of the fathers. (Romans 11:28 NASB)

The Jews currently oppose the gospel. That is what Christians see. God, however, sees Israel's future repentance. They are still his beloved. Should our older brother be anything less to us?

> GOD SEES ISRAEL'S FUTURE REPENTANCE,
>
> AND THEY ARE STILL HIS BELOVED.

Now that we have learned God is not finished with Israel, let's look at the new covenant.

A FOREVER PROMISE

Does the new covenant in Jesus's blood apply to Israel? Romans 11:26–27 mentions the covenant. These verses in Romans are a direct quote of Isaiah 59.

> And so all Israel will be saved; just as it is written, "The Deliverer will come from Zion, he will remove ungodliness from Jacob. This is my covenant with them, when I take away their sins." (Romans 11:26–27 NASB)

This is the covenant Jesus will apply when he returns and forgives Israel's sin. What could this be but the new covenant? Did you notice that this covenant is with Israel, not with the Church? In both the Old Testament and the New Testament God has never made a covenant with the Church; only with Israel. The new covenant applies to the Church because we have been grafted in to the roots of Israel. Let's look at another mention of the new covenant in the Old Testament.

> "Behold, days are coming," declares the Lord, "when *I will make a new covenant with the house of Israel* and with the house of Judah, not like the covenant which I made with their fathers in the day I took them by the hand to bring them out of the land of Egypt, My covenant which they broke, although I was a husband to them," declares the Lord. "But this is the covenant which I will make with the house of Israel after those days," declares the Lord, "I will put My law within them and on their heart I will write it; and I will be their God, and they shall be My people. (Jeremiah 31:31–33 NASB, emphasis mine)

These verses are transparently clear that God was about to make a new covenant with Israel, not the Church. Again, the Church has access to it because they are grafted into Israel. This passage is obviously talking about the new covenant that Jesus ushered in on the cross because it specifically mentions the covenant God made with Moses (the Mosaic covenant) and says the new covenant won't be like the old one.

> THE CHURCH HAS ACCESS TO THE NEW COVENANT BECAUSE IT IS GRAFTED INTO THE ROOTS OF ISRAEL.

Again, this should fill the Church with humility.

THE OTHER PROMISE

We learned the new covenant replaces the Mosaic covenant (the covenant with Moses). These covenants deal with the critically important issue of salvation. But God has made other forever promises with Israel. The promise God made to Abraham about the land of Israel, we call the Abrahamic covenant. It has two main provisions:

- Special favor with God;

  Now the Lord had said to Abram: "Get out of your country, from your family and from your father's house, to a land that I will show you. I will make you a great nation; I will bless you and make your name great; and you shall be a blessing. I will bless those who bless you, and I will curse him who curses you; and in you all the families of the earth shall be blessed." (Genesis 12:1–3 NKJV)

- Land provisions;

  And the Lord said to Abram, after Lot had separated from him: "Lift your eyes now and look from the place where you are—northward, southward, eastward, and westward; for all the land which you see I give to you and your descendants forever." (Genesis 13:14–15 NKJV)

  And it came to pass, when the sun went down and it was dark, that behold, there appeared a smoking oven and a burning torch that passed between those pieces. On the same day the Lord made a covenant with Abram, saying: "To your descendants I have given this land, from the river of Egypt to the great river, the River Euphrates." (Genesis 15:17–18 NKJV)

As can be seen from these passages, the physical land of Israel was given to the Jews. In fact, the land granted extends far beyond the borders of present-day Israel. Those who say the Jews have no right to the land or that the Palestinians have a right to the land don't understand, or they deny, the truth of God's Word. They risk God's wrath because he will bless those who bless Israel and curse those who curse Israel. This is not an idle promise.

> ## IF YOU SAY THE JEWS HAVE NO RIGHT TO THE LAND, YOU DENY THE TRUTH OF GOD'S WORD.

DRY BONES

In addition to these scriptural covenants, the interplay of the history of Israel and prophecy is also amazing confirmation that God is not done with the Jews. It also demonstrates that the Palestinians have no right to the land.

Israel became a nation again in 1948. The intervening years since then have dulled our awareness of what an awesome prophetic event the re-creation of Israel was. At the time, prophecy students were struck by the fulfillment of Ezekiel 37 as the "dry bones" of the nation sprang to life. This was the fulfillment of a number of separate prophecies. The first prophecies involved the dispersion of Israel after their defeat in AD 70 and the subsequent desolation of the land.

> Then the Lord will scatter you among all peoples, from one end of the earth to the other, and there you shall serve other gods, which neither you nor your fathers have known—wood and stone. And among those nations you shall find no rest, nor shall the sole of your foot have a resting place; but there the Lord will give you a trembling heart, failing eyes, and anguish of soul. Your life shall hang in doubt before you; you shall fear day and night, and have no assurance of life. (Deuteronomy 28:64–66 NKJV)

The foreigner who comes from a far land, would say, when they see the plagues of that land and the sicknesses which the Lord has laid on it: "The whole land is brimstone, salt, and burning; it is not sown, nor does it bear, nor does any grass grow there, like the overthrow of Sodom and Gomorrah, Admah, and Zeboiim, which the Lord overthrew in His anger and His wrath." All nations would say, "Why has the Lord done so to this land? What does the heat of this great anger mean?" Then people would say: "Because they have forsaken the covenant of the Lord God of their fathers, which He made with them when He brought them out of the land of Egypt." (Deuteronomy 29:22–25 NKJV, emphasis mine).

In 1867, American author Mark Twain, a foreigner from a far land, wrote about the area in *The Innocents Abroad*:

The further we went the hotter the sun got and the more rocky and bare, repulsive and dreary the landscape became . . . There was hardly a tree or a shrub anywhere. Even the olive and the cactus, those fast friends of a worthless soil, had almost deserted the country. No landscape exists that is more tiresome to the eye than that which bounds the approaches to Jerusalem . . . Jerusalem is mournful, dreary and lifeless. I would not desire to live here. It is a hopeless, dreary, heartbroken land . . . Palestine sits in sackcloth and ashes.

It is said that before the Jews returned to Palestine only about fifteen thousand trees grew in the entire area that would become Israel. During this period a scattered, nomadic people who considered themselves Syrians populated the area. During the four hundred years that Arabs occupied this territory, no attempt was made to create a sovereign Palestinian state. The land was considered worthless.

In 1917, the Balfour Declaration indicated Britain's intention to cede the area currently containing Israel and Jordan to the Jews. Arab outrage at this declaration prompted Britain to create Jordan as the Palestinian Arab state. It is highly interesting that today the world is focused on creating a homeland for the Palestinians when one already exists—the nation of Jordan. In reality, there are no Palestinian people. The area was named Palestine by the Romans to make the world forget Israel. The inhabitants prior to the re-creation of the nation of Israel were Syrians.[28]

The Plowman Overtakes the Reaper

Israel did not remain desolate. First, God began gathering the Jews to Israel and Jerusalem.

> Behold, I will save my people from the land of the east and from the land of the west; I will bring them back, and they shall dwell in the midst of Jerusalem. (Zechariah 8:7–8 NKJV)

Second, God allowed the land to once again produce and be fruitful.

> Behold, the days are coming says the Lord when the plowman shall overtake the reaper and the treader of grapes him who sows seed. The mountains shall drip with sweet wine and all the hills shall flow with it. I will bring back the captives of My people Israel; they shall build the waste cities and inhabit them. They shall plant vineyards and drink wine from them; they shall also make gardens and eat fruit from them. I will plant them in their land and no longer shall they be pulled up. (Amos 9:13–15 NKJV)

Third, God revived the ancient Hebrew language as the official language of Israel after more than 1,800 years.

> For then I will restore to the peoples a pure language that they all may call on the name of the Lord to serve Him with one accord. (Zephaniah 3:9 NKJV)

God also promised controversy over the ownership of Jerusalem would become the focus of world geopolitics.

> Behold, I will make Jerusalem a cup of drunkenness to all the surrounding peoples. (Zechariah 12:2 NKJV)

These are only a small portion of the large number of prophecies fulfilled by the re-creation of Israel as a nation. I encourage you to reread the prophets with this fulfillment in mind.

IRON SCEPTER

The Christmas narrative is one of the most beautiful stories ever told. The incarnation of the Creator of the universe as a humble baby born in a stable speaks volumes about the nature of God. As much as we love this story, it has had a profound negative effect on the Church. We tend to overemphasize God's humility at the expense of his majesty. We tend to forget that although he came as an unassuming infant and held his awesome power in restraint during his first coming, he is returning as both judge and king. He will rule the nations with a rod of iron.

> Ask of Me, and I will surely give the nations as Your inheritance, and the very ends of the earth as Your possession. You shall break them with a rod of iron; You shall shatter them like earthenware. (Psalm 2:8–9 NASB)

This does not seem the same person as the meek and mild Jesus that our Western Church embraces. We have forgotten that he will reign from his glorious throne in Jerusalem. He will be our Jewish king. He is the Lion of the Tribe of Judah; he is not a pussycat from Hollywood. Amen.

> Thus says the Lord, "I will return to Zion and will dwell in the midst of Jerusalem. Then Jerusalem will be called the City of Truth, and the mountain of the Lord of hosts will be called the Holy Mountain." (Zechariah 8:3 NASB)

What will happen to the saints of God in this earthly kingdom?

> Then the sovereignty, the dominion and the greatness of all the kingdoms under the whole heaven will be given to the people of the saints of the Highest One; His kingdom will be an everlasting kingdom, and all the dominions will serve and obey Him. (Daniel 7:27 NASB)

> Do you not know that the saints will judge the world? (1 Corinthians 6:2 NASB)

The Christians and the Jews, who repent and accept Jesus as their Lord and Savior, will judge and rule the nations with Christ! Jerusalem will be the capital of this kingdom, and Jesus will be our king. How can we read these scriptures and still hold a view that God is finished with the Jews?

ONE HOUSEHOLD

Now that we are assured through scripture and history that God is not through with Israel and that God has granted them the land, how are Christians and Jews to interrelate? God tells us that he has created one people, one household out of the Gentile believers and the Jews.

> There is neither Jew nor Greek, there is neither slave nor free man, there is neither male nor female; for you are all one in Christ Jesus. (Galatians 3:28 NASB)

> For by one Spirit we were all baptized into one body, whether Jews or Greeks, whether slaves or free, and we were all made to drink of one Spirit. (1 Corinthians 12:13 NASB)

These familiar passages don't refer only to the ancient past; they refer to the future as well when "all Israel will be saved" and we will be one household in Christ Jesus but still with some distinctives—for example, the Jews will live separately in Israel under David, the prince.

Household Servants

Does God have a special plan for his household in the time before Jesus's return? Does he have a plan for those of us he has set in charge of that household? He certainly does. In chapter two we looked at the illustration of the head of the house and the thief. We saw that the head of the house were Christian leaders. We also learned that if they were watchful they could protect their house (churches) from Satan, who is the thief. Immediately after this illustration, Jesus tells us what makes a faithful leader of his house.

> Who then is the faithful and sensible slave whom his master put in charge of his household to give them their food at the proper time? Blessed is that slave whom his master finds so doing when he comes. Truly I say to you that he will put him in charge of all his possessions. (Matthew 24:45–47 NASB)

This somewhat obscure passage is found in the parable of the faithful and evil slaves. The passage is obscure because the Church hasn't known what to make of it. What the Church has missed is that in verse 45, Jesus is asking us a riddle! He asks, "Who then is the faithful and sensible slave?" A few verses earlier in the Olivet Discourse, Jesus had referred to Noah and compared his return to this Old Testament character. In Luke 17 when speaking to the Pharisees, Jesus compared his return to Lot. Could Jesus be referring to another Old Testament figure here? Here are the clues Jesus gives us:

- The faithful head of his household is a slave;

- He is put in charge of his household by his master;

- He provides food for his household at the appointed time.

Have you guessed the answer yet? It's Joseph! Jesus is telling us to act like Joseph at the appointed time! Let's see how Joseph is the perfect answer to Jesus's riddle:

- His brothers sold Joseph into slavery;

- Potiphar, his master, made him the head of his household and put him in charge of all of his possessions;

- Joseph provided food for both his Jewish brothers and the Egyptians during the seven-year famine.

You may be asking, *How is it possible no one has seen this verse as a riddle before?* The answer is obvious. As we discussed in chapter two, God has sovereignly chosen this time to reveal new revelations to us. It most likely is time for us to take the next step. The follow-up question then is: *How does Jesus want me to be like Joseph?* Let's first look at the reward Jesus promises to those who accomplish his will:

> Blessed is that slave whom his master finds so doing when he comes. Truly I say to you that he will put him in charge of all his possessions. (Matthew 24:46–47 NASB)

Those of us who act like Joseph will be put in charge of all of Jesus's possessions upon his return! When Jesus sits on his glorious throne, those who understand and live out this command will be the leaders of his kingdom. If we are going to accomplish this task, we need to understand who God's household is and what kind of food Jesus is talking about.

We have learned that God's people are Gentiles and Jews. The faithful slave will care for both. Food has a dual meaning here, I believe. Certainly it refers to God's Word. "It is written, 'Man shall not live on bread alone, but on every word that proceeds out of the mouth of God'" (Matthew 4:4 NASB). But I believe Matthew 24:45 also refers to physical bread.

In chapter six, we learned that Jesus foretold there will be famines during the beginning of the birth pangs period. We also saw that once the mark of the Beast is established, no one will be able to buy or sell without it. During that time the Church will face a famine more severe than any

Joseph saw during his lifetime. It is interesting that Jesus's parable refers to the time food will be needed at the "proper time" (the appointed time). The Greek uses *kairos*, which means "a time that has been especially set aside for this purpose." There can be no question that Jesus is referring to the period of time he prophesied in the first half of the Olivet Discourse. It is the same "appointed time of the end" referred to by Daniel in Daniel 8:19: "He said, 'Behold, I am going to let you know what will occur at the final period of the indignation, for it pertains to the appointed time of the end'" (Daniel 8:19 NASB). See how all the pieces fit?

WE ARE TO PROVIDE SPIRITUAL AND PHYSICAL FOOD DURING THE COMING HARD TIMES.

Jesus is telling his faithful servants to be prepared to provide the spiritual food of his Word, and physical food to his household during the hard times that are coming. Does this mean we are to become preppers? Yes, it does. Jesus says so directly—we are to provide his household with food just as Joseph did. Notice, however, the parable doesn't say to provide for our household, it says *his* household. The preppers we have seen in the media are preparing for themselves and their own families. God is calling us to prepare for *his* family, Christians and Jews.

At the conclusion of the Olivet Discourse, Jesus shows how seriously he takes the idea of providing for his household during the tribulation. We call this section of the Olivet Discourse the prophecy of the goats and the sheep.

> Then the King will say to those on His right, "Come, you who are blessed of My Father, inherit the kingdom prepared for you from the foundation of the world. For I was hungry, and you gave Me something to eat; I was thirsty, and you gave Me something to drink; I was a stranger, and you invited Me in;

naked, and you clothed Me; I was sick, and you visited Me; I was in prison, and you came to Me." Then the righteous will answer Him, "Lord, when did we see You hungry, and feed You, or thirsty, and give You something to drink? And when did we see You a stranger, and invite You in, or naked, and clothe You? When did we see You sick, or in prison, and come to You?" The King will answer and say to them, "Truly I say to you, to the extent that you did it to one of these brothers of Mine, even the least of them, you did it to Me." (Matthew 25:34–40 NASB)

During the persecutions of the tribulation, Jesus's household will need food, water, shelter, clothing, and medical attention. Jesus will judge based on how his household is provided for during this very difficult time. This judgment has universal application but has special meaning for the time right before Jesus's return. That is why Jesus included it in the Olivet Discourse. His faithful slaves, who not only provide for his household but understand his Word now and prepare, will be given a special reward.

PROVIDING FOR THE WOMAN

In the book of Revelation we learn that Satan will attempt to destroy the Jews during the tribulation. They will flee from his presence and will escape.

Now a great sign appeared in heaven: a woman clothed with the sun, with the moon under her feet, and on her head a garland of twelve stars. Then being with child, she cried out in labor and in pain to give birth. And another sign appeared in heaven: behold, a great, fiery red dragon having seven heads and ten horns, and seven diadems on his heads. His tail drew a third of the stars of heaven and threw them to the earth. And the dragon stood before the woman who was ready to give birth, to devour her Child as soon as it was born. She bore a male Child who was to rule all nations with a rod of iron. And her Child was caught up to God and His throne. Then the woman fled into the wilderness, where she has a place prepared by God, that they should feed her there one thousand two hundred and sixty days. (Revelation 12:1–6 NKJV)

Most scholars interpret the woman in this passage to mean Israel, the nation who gave birth to Jesus. Some view the woman as Mary. But notice the tense changes at the end of the passage where it says she *has* a place prepared by God. This is present tense. God has the place prepared for her future use, so this is not speaking of the past. This is an example of near/far prophecy, having some past fulfillment as well as a final future fulfillment.

Of greatest interest is the portion of the passage that says "they" should feed her 1,260 days. Who is the *they*? Might it be the faithful slaves who have prepared? Might it be Christians? Might it be you and me?

IN PROVIDING FOR ISRAEL, WE WILL BE JOINING IN THE SALVATION OF THE JEWS.

If we do provide for and hide Israel from Satan, we will have an awesome opportunity to witness to those within our care. In this way we will have the chance to join our Lord in the salvation of the Jews. What an amazing opportunity we may be given!

A HISTORIC FORESHADOW

Is there historic precedent for providing for God's household in time of trouble? There is! During the Holocaust, Christians opened their homes to hide Jews and attempted to help them escape.

The movie *Schindler's List* provides an excellent picture of those times for this generation.

The ten Boom family of Holland is an even more graphic example of providing for God's household. Corrie ten Boom wrote about their efforts in the book *The Hiding Place* (Chosen Books, 1971), which I highly recommend. Corrie's family hid Jews in their home from Nazi persecution and helped some escape. Unfortunately, their neighbors suspected what was occurring and turned the ten Boom family in to the Nazis. On the day the SS came to arrest the ten Booms, they also searched for the Jews they were hiding. The hiding place the ten Booms had constructed in their home did its job and the Jews weren't found. Those in hiding were even able to later escape out of the country.

The ten Booms were not as fortunate. Only Corrie survived the concentration camps. Her father Casper's famous words after being interrogated by the Nazis were, "I would be proud to give my life to save God's chosen people." An elderly man, he survived only ten days of imprisonment.[29]

Another famous Christian from this era was Dietrich Bonhoeffer, a German pastor. Bonhoeffer saw the atrocities that were occurring and fearlessly spoke out against the Nazi regime. This landed him in prison, and later he was hanged in a concentration camp. His encounter with a fellow pastor timelessly speaks to our calling to protect God's household. Bonhoeffer was in prison when a fellow pastor came on a regular visit. Shocked to see Bonhoeffer as a prisoner, the other pastor asked, "Why are you here?" Bonhoeffer replied, "Why aren't you here?" He was implying that the other pastor was not speaking out against the Nazis and in so doing was assisting them.[30]

As church leaders, we all must begin to prepare our minds so that we are ready to act when it is our turn. The Holocaust of the 1940s was only a glimpse of the great holocaust to come. How will we react when given the chance to stand up for the Jews? Will we look the other way? Will Jesus judge us as sheep or goats?

THE SECRET PLACE

Psalm 91 talks about the secret place of the Most High that has been a refuge for believers throughout the ages of the Church. This special psalm promises God's protection in times of trouble. Millions have turned to it for strength and encouragement. Close examination of the words of this psalm show it has special meaning for the "time of Jacob's trouble" (the tribulation). Might we be utilized by God to provide the secret place for the Jews during this time? Might God provide one for us as well, later when the Antichrist turns on the Christians (Revelation 12:17)?

The answers to the questions above are not yet clear, but it is an important psalm to understand. This is a wonderful scripture to memorize to use in time of trouble. A famine of God's Word is coming (Amos 8:11–12). There will be a day when the only scripture we have to guide us and comfort us is what we have memorized or that we hide in our shoes. (In the concentration camp, the ten Booms famously hid pages torn from their Bible in their shoes.)

Our times are not yet that desperate; let's take a look at the Psalm.

> He who dwells in the secret place of the Most High shall abide under the shadow of the Almighty. I will say of the Lord, "He is my refuge and my fortress; My God, in Him I will trust. (Psalm 91:1–2 NKJV)

I have always been fascinated with the concept of a secret place. In Hebrew the word means "the hidden place, the hiding place, the covered place, or the covert place." It is mentioned numerous times in scripture. Psalm 27 speaks specifically of the secret place during time of trouble.

> For in the time of trouble He shall hide me in His pavilion; in the secret place of His tabernacle He shall hide me; He shall set me high upon a rock. (Psalm 27:5 NKJV)

Psalm 31 is also specific about hiding us from the conspiracies of men. This passage reminds me of Psalm 2 when the nations rage against God and his Messiah.

> You shall hide them in the secret place of Your presence from the plots of man; you shall keep them secretly in a pavilion from the strife of tongues. (Psalm 31:20 NKJV)

SHADOW OF THE ALMIGHTY

Although we may dwell in the secret place, we shall *abide* in the shadow of the Almighty. The Hebrew word translated "shadow" means "under the protection of." Some scriptures picture this type of protection as the shelter provided by a roof. Other more intimate analogies show a mother bird's wings covering her young. All of these are pictures of how God will protect us, his people, at that time before Jesus's return.

In Isaiah is a very special picture of how God hid Jesus in the shadow of his hand until he was ready for ministry.

> And he has made My mouth like a sharp sword; *in the shadow of His hand He has hidden Me*, and made Me a polished shaft; in His quiver He has hidden Me. (Isaiah 49:2 NKJV, emphasis mine)

I believe, in the same way, God's hand might hide his people from the Antichrist. Despite all the drones and GPS systems available, God's hand can block and frustrate the Antichrist, making him unable to hunt down the elect. However, even in martyrdom, if that is what he has called us to, he has promised to be with us always, even to the end of the age (Matthew 28:20).

THE SECRET PLACE IS HIS PRESENCE

God's presence is the safest possible place to be. I don't believe we need to begin scouting out mountain retreats in which to hide. If God desires us to hide at that time, we might be given eagles' wings (Revelation 12:14; Exodus 19:4; Isaiah 40:31). What we do need to do immediately, however, is to place all our trust in God alone. "He is my refuge and my fortress; My God, in Him I will trust" (Psalm 91:2 NKJV). God is our fortress whether he hides us or walks with us to face our adversary. Either way, we are completely safe with him. Eternity with him is our perspective no matter what happens to us on earth before he comes.

WE ARE COMPLETELY SAFE WITH GOD.

SUMMARY

We have seen that many in the Christian Church believe God is done with Israel and the Jews and that the Church is now the beneficiary of God's promises in the Old Testament. Unfortunately, this mistaken belief is a source of anti-Semitic and anti-Zionist attitudes. God's Word, however, clearly demonstrates that God has a wonderful plan of salvation for Israel and the Jews.

We discovered that God also has a plan for Christians to act like Joseph in the appointed time before Jesus's return to provide for both Christians and Jews. We all need to ask God to show us how he desires us to proceed in accomplishing this command.

The basic steps for getting ready for Jesus from this chapter are:

1. Israel plays a key role in God's plan for Jesus's return:
   God plans to redeem a remnant of the Jews. Someday all of Israel will be saved.

2. The land of Israel has been given to the Jews by God:
   We must avoid the deception that the Palestinians have a right to the land.

3. God will bless those that bless Israel:
   We should pray for and support Israel and the Jews.

4. God's household are the Christians and the Jews:
   We are brothers and must support them in their time of trouble.

5. We are to act like Joseph in the appointed time:
   God wants us to provide spiritual and physical food for the Jews during the tribulation.

In the epilogue, I'll give you my sense of what God wants us to do with our newfound knowledge that we have gained in the first seven chapters.

EPILOGUE

AN UNLIKELY CHOICE:
WHAT'S THE NEXT STEP?

The horse is made *ready* for the day of battle, but victory rests with the Lord. (Proverbs 21:31 NIV, emphasis mine)

In chapter one of this book, we presented a thesis that preparing for the return of Jesus involves much more than a simple profession of faith. Throughout chapters two through seven, we built on that thesis and demonstrated what God's Word has to say about preparation. Hopefully, although you may have found aspects of this teaching radical and contrary to much of what the Church has traditionally believed, you have also seen that the big picture we present is amazingly consistent within itself and consistent to the testimony of scripture.

In these chapters, we have seen how the Church is asleep in regard to many facets of Jesus's return, just as he prophesied it would be. We also learned that this slumber and a lack of understanding of what Jesus's return is really about is dangerous, and how hundreds of millions of churchgoers are at risk of falling away in the great apostasy that is coming.

We have now reached the concluding section of the book, and it is time to pull all the pieces together. God desires that we not only understand his Word, but also that we apply it. "But prove yourselves doers of the word, and not merely hearers who delude themselves" (James 1:22 NASB). Hearing is always so much easier than doing, especially if you feel unqualified. In chapter one of this book, we mentioned unlikely choices. As I mentioned in that chapter, I was an unlikely choice to write this book. Like me, you may also feel you are an unlikely choice to accomplish something earthshaking for God.

The topic of unlikely choices reminds me of one of my favorite preachers. His name was Johnny, and he was more than a bit eccentric. If there ever was an unlikely choice to accomplish something for God, Johnny was it. You see, Johnny was homeless and to the best of my knowledge never preached inside a church building. He would rather sit out in the open and let his congregation come to him. Even after he became famous and could have easily started his own church, Johnny chose to be homeless. He scavenged for food and wore clothing that labeled him as a bum. Frankly, Johnny didn't care what people thought about him. He only cared what God thought about him.

Johnny's message was different as well. His sermons weren't a watered down, let's-not-offend gospel. Johnny never took an offering and didn't care if two folks or two hundred came to hear him preach. Money didn't motivate him, and neither did attendance. But people would cram around him in all kinds of weather to hear messages that most big-time preachers were afraid to deliver. He didn't tailor his message to what folks wanted to hear; he told it like it was, and maybe that was his attraction. Johnny wasn't afraid to call out frauds, either. He made it his business to expose the self-righteous, prosperity preachers in town. He frequently blasted politicians as well for their decadent lifestyles. Needless to say, Johnny spent a fair amount of time in jail. There is a price to pay for exposing the rich and famous. He was an incredibly unlikely choice, but God used him mightily.

Every ministry has a defining moment, and Johnny's had his. One day his cousin came to hear him preach. When Johnny saw his cousin, he was overwhelmed and uttered these famous words, "Behold the Lamb of God!" Well, now you probably realize who Johnny was. We all refer to him by the name John the Baptist. About him Jesus said:

> Truly I say to you, among those born of women there has not
> arisen anyone greater than John the Baptist! Yet the one who

is least in the kingdom of heaven is greater than he. (Matthew 11:11 NASB)

Did you catch that last part of what Jesus said? He told us that the least likely in his kingdom would be even greater than John the Baptist. Friend, that means you and I can be the ones Jesus was talking about. I certainly am an unlikely choice, and I bet if you look at yourself, you are too. I believe God prefers to use the unlikely. Being an unlikely choice may actually be an advantage. When an amazingly talented person brings God's Word or serves God in another capacity, sometimes it's the person who gets the glory. When an untalented person serves God, God receives the glory. Only the anointing of God's Spirit can explain why an untalented person can communicate God's Word or effectively perform service for God.

JOHN THE BAPTIST'S "LIFE VERSE"

Obedience is all God needed from John the Baptist. John's calling was expressed in this simple verse:

> He said, "I am a voice of one crying in the wilderness, 'MAKE STRAIGHT THE WAY OF THE LORD,' as Isaiah the prophet said." (John 1:23 NASB)

John's call was to help prepare his world for the first coming of Jesus. In his day, when a great dignitary was to visit a city, he would send a representative to let everyone know he was coming. In addition to proclaiming the dignitary was coming, this representative would also get the road ready for the chariot of the dignitary. Because most roads were made of dirt in those days, the representative sometimes had to fill potholes and level out humps in the road. John was the voice crying in the wilderness of the sin and corruption that was first-century Judah. Before our Messiah came, John preached to help fill in the potholes of sin in his listeners' lives and to also knock down those who felt high and mighty. His mission was to make straight the way of the Lord at his first coming.

I believe Jesus is calling us in twenty-first-century America to be voices crying in the wilderness as well. He wants us to make straight the way for Jesus's return before his second coming. Our mission is modeled on John's. We don't have to be homeless and live as John did, but God desires the same level of dedication John showed. Talent and skill are not the most important attributes to have. It primarily requires a love of God and obedience.

COMFORT, YES!

John's life verse was a quote from Isaiah the prophet. Most readers probably think this famous verse is a direct quote of John's, but it isn't. It's from the Old Testament. This is a fascinating piece of scripture at which I think we all should take a look.

> Comfort, yes, comfort My people!" says your God. "Speak comfort to Jerusalem, and cry out to her, that her warfare is ended, that her iniquity is pardoned; for she has received from the Lord's hand double for all her sins." The voice of one crying in the wilderness: "Prepare the way of the Lord; Make straight in the desert a highway for our God. Every valley shall be exalted and every mountain and hill brought low; the crooked places shall be made straight and the rough places smooth; *the glory of the Lord shall be revealed, and all flesh shall see it together;* for the mouth of the Lord has spoken." (Isaiah 40:1–5 NKJV, emphasis mine)

Do you see that last verse? "The glory of the Lord shall be revealed, and all flesh shall see it together." This has not happened yet—at Jesus's first coming, everyone did not see his glory. Hence, this fulfillment is ultimately in the future. God's glory will be revealed, and indeed all flesh shall see it when Christ returns at his second coming. That means this famous life verse of John the Baptist applies even more to us today than it did to John. It was partially fulfilled in John's day, but its final fulfillment will most probably be with us and our generation. I highly recommend you read this entire chapter of Isaiah 40 and pray and meditate about what it means for each of us.

I could write an entire book about this section of scripture, but for now I would like to look at one verse in particular, the first one. "'Comfort, yes, comfort my people!' says your God" (Isaiah 40:1 NKJV).

When we speak of the return of Jesus, when we prepare the way of the Lord, people's initial reaction will always be fear. That is why God's first command in Isaiah 40 is to "comfort, yes, comfort my people." God does not desire for us to fear. His perfect love wants to drive out all fear. Satan is the one who wants to scare us. Peter tells us Satan is a roaring lion. So, if you're scared by the thought of Jesus's return, remember who it is that is making you afraid. It isn't Jesus. His desire and overwhelming passion is to comfort his people regarding his return.

People have a number of different fears. Some have read about horrible things happening prior to Jesus's return. Others love their current lives so much they want to hang on to the status quo just a little longer. Some churches avoid speaking about Jesus's return because they fear their congregations will stop attending.

But the overriding idea that Jesus wants to leave with all of us is this: He is coming back! Jesus changes everything. As we discussed in chapter four, what we are experiencing now is nothing compared to what will be. All of creation has been made for that exact moment when Jesus appears on this earth. The joy we will experience will be unbelievable. Remember, we will be caught up in the air together with our loved ones, our friends, and fellow believers to meet Jesus and let him take us to heaven with him. We are going to experience this as a family, both the living and those who have passed on. And best of all, Jesus will be with us. Any small suffering or sacrifice will be nothing compared to that. Any small loss here on earth—not seeing our grandchildren born, never getting married, never seeing Hawaii, etc.—will be nothing compared to being with Jesus and all the believers.

This is what all creation is groaning for. This was also the focus of all the biblical prophets. They primarily wrote about the day of the Lord, the coming of the Messiah, and his eternal kingdom. The events prior to his return are important, but they shouldn't be our ultimate focus.

The focus of the Church needs to be on Jesus's glorious return and being with him in his kingdom.

> ## FOCUS ON JESUS AND HIS RETURN,
> ## AND COMFORT HIS PEOPLE.

As you move forward into the ministry that I know God will give you to prepare for his return, remember to comfort his people.

THE NEXT STEP

One of the reasons NASA officials chose Neil Armstrong to be the first man to walk on the moon was that he didn't have a big ego. Out of all the astronauts participating in the Apollo program, Armstrong was the most likely to be able to handle the social pressure that would follow his first steps. Standing on the ladder of the lunar module, he hopped into the alien gravity of the moon and onto its dusty surface uttering these famous words, "That's one small step for [a] man; one giant leap for mankind." All of America assumed he planned his statement long in advance, but Armstrong, in his typical humble fashion, made it up on the spot. In an interview after he returned to earth, he told a reporter that he considered the lunar landing very risky with only a 50 percent chance of success. He was concentrating all his effort on the touchdown. What he would say after they landed was the last thing on his mind. Twenty minutes after Armstrong's first step, Buzz Aldrin became the second human to walk on the moon, and a new era of endeavor had begun.

The first step in any new direction is always the most difficult. Inertia and anxiety must be overcome. We resist change. But God is doing a new thing. The time of the end has begun with the re-creation of the nation of Israel in 1948. If we are to walk alongside Jesus, we must change as well. It was no different with his first coming. Only John the Baptist saw what God was doing ("Behold the Lamb of God"). The religious leaders of that day were full of major misconceptions about the promised Messiah and what he would do. Should we be surprised that today, during the advent of his second coming, conditions are essentially the same? The established religious leaders are still beset by major misconceptions. They are asleep.

On my personal spiritual walk, my first step was to set my face toward Jerusalem—to mentally accept the fact that God's will for me would take me places I might not always choose to go on my own. It would require sacrifices I wouldn't choose to make individually. I realized immediately that walking this path would place me in opposition with the established Church that may not want to change its views of Jesus's return. It is difficult for an individual to change; it is extremely difficult for an institution to change.

If you accept the role God has called you to, you may face opposition from your church and its leadership and perhaps even the government. John the Baptist accepted his role and its consequences. He is our model for how to prepare the way of the Lord. That is our call, after all.

You will also face uncertainty. The revelations in the book may have surprised you. What other new revelations does the Lord have for us? I think God likes a certain amount of uncertainty—it requires faith, and only faith can please God!

We must try to hold our own ideas of Jesus's return loosely and seek God constantly throughout the process. God has given us only enough information for us to take the next step. This is God's standard operating principle. We are to walk by faith, not sight.

God Chooses His Army

In the Old Testament, Gideon was the poster child of uncertainty. God had chosen him to deliver Israel from the Midianites. The Midianite army numbered 135,000, while the Israelites had 32,000 men. The Lord's comment to Gideon about this mismatch is one of my favorite verses in the Bible:

> The people who are with you are *too many* for Me to give Midian into their hands. (Judges 7:2 NASB, emphasis mine)

Gideon must have thought, *Too many? We are outnumbered four to one!* But God's will is utterly independent of natural laws. While Gideon looked at physical numbers, God looks at the hearts of those he uses for his glory. Not only would God get the glory from the victory, but God desired the right men to accomplish his mission. He saw many who were unfit for the task before them.

Perhaps it is the same in the ministry of awakening the Church. Soldiers with the wrong spirit will only get in the way.

God's first layoff in choosing Gideon's army was based on fear. Two-thirds of Gideon's force left because they were afraid. I anticipate that at least two-thirds of the church leaders approached will have nothing to do with this ministry because they will be afraid to take a stand on the return of Jesus. We should not fear this layoff. God is choosing his army.

Next, God made a strange request. He asked Gideon to lead his men to the water and watch how they drank. Those who cupped their fingers and drank from their hands were to be retained. All those who lapped up the water directly from the stream were excused from service. Only three hundred men drank from their hands and remained.

What does this mean? It has a direct correlation to this ministry. Those who drank from their hands were able to remain watchful. Their eyes were not fixed on the water around them, but rather they scanned the horizon while their hands held the water. Those who lapped up the water from the source took their eyes off events around them. God's command for all of us before Jesus's return is to watch.

Only those keeping a watch on the events prophetically unfolding will be helpful to God in this endeavor. This is how God will choose his army.

So, what is *your* next step? Only God can determine your path. *"A man's heart plans his way, but the* Lord *directs his steps* (Proverbs 16:9 NKJV). Pray and seek God's will. The oil of the Holy Spirit will guide you.

Transforming Concepts

Gideon's foes were the Midianites who were ravishing the land of Israel. In Hebrew, Midian means *strife*. Gideon famously overcame their army of over 100,000 with only three hundred soldiers. At night Gideon's men carried trumpets and torches concealed in jars of clay. On Gideon's command, they broke the jars to expose the light and blew the trumpets. Shocked and confused, the army of Midian (strife) fought against each other.

You and I are broken jars of clay; we're unlikely choices. Yet we contain within us the brilliant light of the Holy Spirit. When he shines out from within us, we are a mighty army blowing God's warning trumpets. Much can be accomplished with God's help.

At the beginning of this epilogue we saw a quote from Proverbs.

> The horse is made *ready* for the day of battle, but victory rests with the Lord. (Proverbs 21:31 NIV, emphasis mine)

Preparation for battle is our responsibility. Success is God's responsibility. That is why getting ready for Jesus's return is so important: it's our responsibility. God won't do it for us. He will assist us with his Spirit, but we must initiate the action.

In this book, we have looked at six crucial concepts. Allow the Lord to transform you through what you have learned about these concepts, and then share the message.

- **The Church is asleep.** We are to wake them up.
- **The gospel is our treasure.** We are to share the good news of his first *and* second coming.

- **We're to adjust our attitude.** We are to rejoice, send tons of invitations, act like it's the two-minute warning, and keep ourselves pure for our bridegroom.

- **We are not to believe popular prophecy myths.** We must resist the urge to believe date setters and those who teach a theology that we won't see hard times.

- **We are to watch for the signs of Jesus's return** and act appropriately when we see them.

- **We are to bless and support our brother Jacob** (Israel and the Jews).

God desires that we join him in his work. He wants to share this task with us because he loves us. He wants to bless us with the fruit of this ministry. But the hard work of preparation is our responsibility.

IF YOU ARE A PASTOR

The task ahead of you is a tough one. Right now your shepherd's heart may be breaking for your flock, and your leader's mind is asking, *How can this be done?* Awakening a congregation is a challenging task, and the risks are high. But the risks of not addressing this issue are catastrophic. I am praying for you. Feel free to contact me at nelson@AreWeReadyForJesus. com if you need someone to talk to. Our ministry will make resources available to you: books, small group studies, and speakers if desired.

Your first task will be to convince your elders, board, and denomination of the validity of this message. Please contact us if you need encouragement and help preparing.

IF YOU ARE NOT A PASTOR

If the Church is sleeping, we are to wake them gently! Remember, "Comfort, yes comfort my people." Pastors are the heads of God's house on earth. They are the keys to awakening the Church. If the heads of the house are sleeping, the thief can break in and rob. We must awaken as many pastors as we can, as quickly as we can.

How Can We Do This?

Ready for Jesus Ministries (www.AreWeReadyForJesus.com) is dedicated to awakening the Church. We help equip folks like you and me to meet with pastors one-on-one in cities throughout the USA and Canada. We also help pastors bring this challenging message to their denominations, elders, and boards. Is this a demanding job? Yes. It may be like awakening a soundly sleeping prizefighter—dangerous if not done correctly. Thank God, he is the one who does the awakening.

An undertaking like this, obviously, cannot happen without a covering of prayer. Both prayer and fasting are recommended. Can everyone participate? Everyone has a pastor. Everyone can pray. Some can go further and meet with other pastors in their towns. Some can meet a different pastor weekly, or different pastors a few times a month. I am praying that you get involved. Awakening the Church is the primary thing that must be accomplished. Millions of souls, maybe hundreds of millions, are at stake; it is an important and timely ministry.

Final Thoughts

Gideon's army was organized into three companies, numbering one hundred each. Joseph in Egypt collected food and provisions on a city-by-city basis. These ancient role models suggest organization of effort. If you feel so led of the Lord, please e-mail us and let us know that you are on the team. We already have brothers and sisters from many nations dedicated to following God where he leads.

A prophet often has no honor in his hometown. Noah was laughed at as he built a boat in the middle of the wilderness where it had never rained. Even Jesus, who was much more than a prophet, was not accepted in his hometown of Nazareth.

I am praying for each of you to accomplish the difficult task of overcoming in your own church and community. This will be the most difficult task of all. But Jesus will walk with each of us. He said, "Lo, I am with you always, even to the end of the age" (Matthew 28:20 NASB). Might I add, especially at the end of the age? He will not leave us to accomplish this alone.

In chapter one and in this epilogue we discussed why God may use someone who is "unqualified" and an unlikely choice to accomplish his will. I realize we all may feel unqualified; I certainly feel that I am. Why did God pass by more gifted workers and choose us? Probably, because we met his requirements: we were unafraid and "drank from our hands." Let us prepare the way of the Lord together. He is coming soon. Amen.

JOIN THE MOVEMENT TO

AWAKEN THE CHURCH:

READY FOR JESUS MINISTRIES

WWW.AREWEREADYFORJESUS.COM

NELSON@AREWEREADYFORJESUS.COM

Endnotes

Chapter Two

1. "The Didache, c. 50AD – 120AD," *Pre-Wrath Rapture.com*, last modified September 26, 2011, accessed January 18, 2015, http://pre-wrathrapture.com/the-didache/.

2. "Bible Study: The Thief in the Night vs. The Thief," Calvary Bible Church, last modified January 8, 2011, accessed December 23, 2014, http://www.cbcmidway.org/2011/01/08/bible-study-the-thief-in-the-night-vs-the-thief/.

Chapter Three

3. "Talent (measurement)," *Wikipedia*, last modified December 22, 2014, accessed December 23, 2014, http://en.wikipedia.org/wiki/Talent_%28measurement%29.

4. "If Economic Cycle Theorists Are Correct 2015 to 2020 Will Be Pure Hell for The United States," *The Economic Collapse Blog*, accessed October 1, 2014, http://theeconomiccollapseblog.com/archives/if-economic-cycle-theorists-are-correct-2015-to-2020-will-be-pure-hell-for-the-united-states.

5. Ibid.

6. "The Purpose Driven Life," *Wikipedia*, last modified December 22, 2014, accessed December 23, 2014, http://en.wikipedia.org/wiki/The_Purpose_Driven_Life.

Chapter Four

7. "The Unreached," *One World Missions*, accessed December 23, 2014, http://oneworldmissions.com/site.cfm?PageID=6064.

8. Ibid.

9. "US Wars in Afghanistan, Iraq to Cost $6 Trillion," *Global Research News*, last modified September 20, 2013, accessed October 1, 2014, http://www.globalresearch.ca/us-wars-in-afghanistan-iraq-to-cost-6-trillion/5350789.

10. "Over 1 Million Troops Have Fought in Iraq and Afghanistan," *Democratic Underground*, last modified November 27, 2006, accessed October 1, 2014, http://www.democraticunderground.com/discuss/duboard.php?az=view_all&address=364x2814351.

11. "Student Volunteer Movement," *Wikipedia*, last modified December 22, 2014, accessed December 23, 2014, http://en.wikipedia.org/wiki/Student_Volunteer_Movement.

Chapter Five

12. "The Late Great Planet Earth," *Wikipedia*, last modified December 22, 2014, accessed December 23, 2014, http://en.wikipedia.org/wiki/The_Late,_Great_Planet_Earth.

13. Ibid.

14. "Predictions and Claims for the Second Coming of Christ," *Wikipedia*, last modified December 22, 2014, accessed December 23, 2014, http://en.wikipedia.org/wiki/Predictions_and_claims_for_the_Second_Coming_of_Christ.

15. "Isaac Newton," *Wikipedia*, last modified December 22, 2014, accessed December 23, 2014, http://en.m.wikipedia.org/wiki/Isaac_Newton%27s_religious_views.

16. "Predictions and Claims for the Second Coming of Christ," *Wikipedia*.

17. "Left Behind," *Wikipedia*, last modified December 22, 2014, accessed December 23, 2014, http://en.wikipedia.org/wiki/Left_Behind.

18. "Ruth B. Graham on the Pretribulation Rapture," *Ted Montgomery.com*, accessed December 23, http://tedmontgomery.com/bblovrvw/rapture/ruth.html.

19. "Corrie ten Boom on the Tribulation and the Rapture," *Ted Mongomery.com*, accessed December 24, 2014, http://www.tedmontgomery.com/bblovrvw/Rapture/corrie.html.

20. "Rapture," Wikipedia, last modified December 22, 2014, accessed December 23, 2014, http://en.wikipedia.org/wiki/Rapture.

21 "646-apostasia" Bible Hub, last modified: unknown, accessed February 23, 2015, http://biblehub.com/greek/646.htm

22 Ibid.

23. "Corrie ten Boom on the Tribulation and the Rapture," *Ted Mongomery.com*.

Chapter Six

24. "Imminence and the Rapture," Dr. Thomas Ice, accessed October 1, 2014, http://www.pmiministries.com/Literature/Imminence_and_the_Rapture.pdf.

25. "On the origin of the Name Daesh-the Islamic State in Iraq and as Sham," Pieter van Ostaeyen, last modified February 18, 2014, accessed October 1, 2014, http://pietervanostaeyen.wordpress.com/2014/02/18/on-the-origin-of-the-name-daesh-the-islamic-state-in-iraq-and-as-sham/.

26. "Jesus in Islam," *Wikipedia*, last modified December 22, 2014, accessed December 23, 2014, http://en.wikipedia.org/wiki/Jesus_in_Islam.

Chapter Seven

27. "Jimmy Carter to Headline Fundraiser for Hamas Front Group," *Newsmax*, last modified August 28, 2014, accessed October 1, 2014, http://www.newsmax.com/Newsfront/Jimmy-Carter-Fundraiser-Hamas/2014/08/28/id/591451/.

28. "Balfour Declaration," *Wikipedia*, last modified December 22, 2014, accessed December 23, 2014, http://en.wikipedia.org/wiki/Balfour_Declaration.

29. "Casper Ten Boom," *Wikipedia*, last modified December 22, 2014, accessed December 23, 2014, http://en.wikipedia.org/wiki/Casper_ten_Boom.

30. "Dietrich Bonhoeffer," *Wikipedia*, last modified December 22, 2014, accessed December 23, 2014, http://en.wikipedia.org/wiki/Dietrich_Bonhoeffer.